Out of the Fury

The Incredible Odyssey of Eliezer Urbach

As Told to Edith S. Weigand

Cover Design by Janet Myers

National Agent: REF Publishing (703) 631-1115.

ISBN 0-9618904-0-1

First Edition

10   9   8   7   6   5

Printed in the United States of America

The type for this book was set by REF Publishing in 11 point Garamond on 13 points of lead and the book was printed in the United States of America on paper meeting ALA standards.

Table of Contents

Foreword

I met Eliezer Urbach in Tel Aviv in April of 1961. It was the Sabbath of Passover week. I had been invited to speak to the Messianic Assembly. Eliezer Urbach was one of the leaders of the congregation. He was a man of repute among the brethren. In the midst of a hostile environment, he had brought up his children in the nurture and admonition of the Lord. Eliezer's public baptism in the Sea of Jaffa was a courageous testimony, at which the Hebrew Christians boldly demonstrated their faith in the Lord Jesus Christ.

The next day, well-stocked with Passover goodies prepared by Sara, Eliezer's wife, I had my first tour of Jerusalem. Eliezer not only knew and loved Jerusalem, he knew and loved the people. I learned much about Jerusalem, its history, and its people that day, but I also learned to know and love a unique servant of our Lord. Eliezer has suffered much but his adversities did not embitter him, they enabled him to become a sensitive servant of our Lord.

Eliezer means, "God is helper." Eliezer Urbach is well-named. He has demonstrated the truth of his name to multitudes of Jews and Gentiles.

Daniel Fuchs, Chairman
Board of Directors
Chosen People Ministries

Introduction

I didn't know you, Lord, but you knew me.
I didn't love you, but you loved me.
I wasn't searching for you, but you were
searching for me.
Thank you, Lord, for giving me a sense of
your hand on my life. I pray that this
story may glorify your Name.

Eliezer Urbach
Summer, 1986

Preface

In 1971, someone suggested that I write my life story. A young student journalist, Richelle Cross, began the initial interviewing and produced the first rough draft. The embryo manuscript lay in a desk drawer for ten years. I had no desire to dredge up all those painful memories that had taken so many years to seal away in a dark corner of my mind. Why relive the nightmares of the past?

Eventually, the aging paperwork was found by Edith Weigand, who came to do volunteer office work. She urged me to take up writing the book again, for the reason that every personal record of the Nazi reign of terror is needful and important, lest we forget soon that the veneer of civilization is treacherously thin as long as human hearts resist regeneration. We must not allow the passage of time to reduce the Holocaust to a paragraph or two in the encyclopedias.

A Baptist pastor with whom I discussed the matter proceeded to edit the existing material into an abbreviated version. A small portion of this condensed copy was published in **Eternity** magazine, but the full story awaited the effort of my volunteer secretary, who finally pressed me into completing the manuscript.

I wish to express my gratitude to all of the people who contributed to the publication of my life story, to Richelle, and to my pastor friend, Harry Adams, and especially to Edith Weigand, who spent five years gathering details from my reluctant memory, organizing the material into book form, and patiently re-typing the manuscript through many revisions. Without her perseverance, there would be no book.

Most of all, I thank God that there is a life story to write. Driven from my homeland, and orphaned by the forces of evil, I looked for a city, a place of peace and safety somewhere on this earth. I wandered for more years than I care to remember, not only from city to city, but from country to country, until I arrived, by the grace of God, in the spiritual homeland promised to my ancestors in the faith.

I do not mean to sound presumptuous or to claim special election. Most, if not all, of the survivors of the Holocaust wonder why they lived through it while so many millions of others did not. To my knowledge, the question never finds a satisfactory answer. While my own survival through the dark and terrible years of Nazi madness and its aftermath remains a mystery to me, I can truly say that the winds of adversity drove me into an unexpected port. My life was saved many times in many ways during the years encompassed in this story, but none of my physical escapes from death compare with the miracle wrought by God in the heart of this wandering Jew.

Heiman and Berta Urbach

Eliezer and his Catholic nanny

Eliezer Urbach   Ernest Urbach

Ernest, Heiman, and Eliezer Urbach

x

CHAPTER 1

Enroute to the Past

May 9, 1986. After a hectic week of final preparations, I am settled down in my seat, and the United DC-10 has made its ascent to cruising altitude on the way to Kennedy International Airport. Sara saw me to the boarding gate at Stapleton, giving me the usual wifely barrage of last minute instructions and warnings.

The Chernobyl nuclear power plant accident on April 26, and the radiation fallout cloud drifting over my native country, added to the concern of my family and friends about this trip to Poland. Some strongly urged me to cancel the journey. After all, it would be decidedly ironic if the Poles and Russians "got me" forty years after my flight from those territories now threatened by a silent, invisible dust of unknown lethal effects.

Frankly, the "cloud" could not have deterred my departure to revisit my homeland unless travel to the Continent had been prohibited. I had come to believe that God's hand was in the venture, and I trusted that if so, whatever awaited me in Poland was in His providence. As Esther said of her mission to the Persian king to ask that her people be spared, "If I perish, I perish!"

I adjust my seat back, and gaze blankly through the window

of the plane. The sun is already setting behind us, and the clouds below are tinged with pink and purple from the disappearing rays of that royal star. The serene panorama, together with the steady drone of the motors, quiet my pounding pulse, and the excitement of getting off on this adventure, which had taken weeks of preparation, begins to subside.

I could not help but have some mixed feelings about going back to Poland. My feet had not been on native soil since 1945. A kaleidoscope of memories flood my mind—scenes from my happy childhood in Skoczow, the inn at the crossroads where I was born and raised, the rolling green fields that surrounded the farm houses, the beautiful mountains in the distance. What was it the poet observed, "the child is father to the man?" Such an idyllic beginning I had! Manhood was forced upon me abruptly at seventeen years of age, when the Nazis invaded Poland in the Fall of 1939.

The pleasant memories evaporate as I think of that, and other dark scenes take form in the mirror of my mind. The sky outside has turned to night, and the window of the plane reflects only my own face—sixtyish, gray beard, balding head, deep-set, weary eyes. Would anyone in Skoczow recognize Eliezer Urbach, the native son who left for good over 40 years ago? What awaited me on this return? Was it really God's will that I should go back?

The last question, of course, had already been answered or I would never be on this flight. Going back to Poland to be immersed in painful memories that took years to heal would not have been a personal choice. I mentally review one more time the events that led to the journey into my past, as though I needed the confirmation that a genuine call had been made, and whatever came of it had a sanction of its own beyond my comprehension or planning.

Two years ago, an old friend, Mrs. Koffsman, a missionary for thirty years in Jerusalem, came to the United States to a Messianic Conference which I was also attending in Pennsylvania. As we visited, Mrs. Koffsman told me of a premonition she had, confirmed, she believed, in prophetic Scripture.

"Jews are going to make a mass exodus from Russia some time in the near future," she said. "Did you know, Eliezer, that Christians in Finland, Poland, and other European countries are preparing food, clothing, and lodging to receive the influx of Jewish people from Russia when this happens?"

"No, Sister Koffsman, I was not aware either of this expectation or the activity in preparation for such an event. Interesting. Must be widely believed in Europe."

"Yes, it is. Someone has even dubbed the coming phenomenon 'Exodus II.' Eliezer, you need to go to Poland to prepare the churches for this surge of Jewish people into the country."

The business of the Conference was called to order before I had time to assimilate this news from a far country, and I did not see my friend again to continue our conversation. The idea sounded rather far-fetched to me at the time, and I forgot about it for a year and a half—until one day a letter came from Poland.

A Christian woman whom I had never met, wrote me an extraordinary story. By some manner, the lady had received the ABMJ Calendar edition in which my testimony was printed. The brief testimony mentioned that I was born in Skoczow. Because she lived in the same area, the lady suggested in her letter that I return for a visit there, and perhaps speak in the churches. I wrote her the answer that "if God works it out, I will come."

The third unrelated incident, I now recall enroute to my past, occurred at a local church in Denver. After I finished speaking to the congregation one Sunday evening, a fellow approached and introduced himself to me. Then he offered some information.

"A lady is coming from Poland tomorrow, Mr. Urbach. I think you should meet her."

"Very well, it would be my pleasure to visit with someone so recently from Poland. I have been out of touch for a long time. Can you arrange a meeting with her?"

"I certainly can. She will be staying with friends of ours. Here is the number to call. Mrs. S.[1] will no doubt have some interesting things to say to you. I'll tell her to expect to hear from you."

An appointment was made for the following afternoon. When Mrs. S. answered the doorbell, I gave her the traditional Polish-Christian greeting which I remembered from long ago.

"Praise be the name of Jesus Christ!"

"Forever and ever!" Mrs. S. completed the ancient response, patterned after the practice of early believers who used it to establish the identity of a Christian household upon entering a home.

The traditional greeting served to break the ice immediately, and Mrs. S. knew where I stood without preliminary questions. What she proceeded to tell me was indeed exciting information, and on top of it, I received the third invitation to return to Poland for a visiting and guest-speaking tour in and around my home territory.

I learned from Mrs. S. that there are Christian people in her country who are concerned about the remnant of Polish Jews, and that the physical and spiritual needs of some Jewish people, particularly the old and sick among them, are being lovingly provided by these caring Christians.

I could hardly believe my ears as this lady from Poland described the work being done in behalf of my people. When I see it later, I am even more astounded at what hearts full of compassion are able to accomplish when those hearts are inspired and directed by the Lord. Before our initial visit is over, this extraordinary lady repeated the same message.

"Eliezer, please come to Poland to visit your Jewish brethren and speak to our Christian congregations. As a Jewish believer, you can help build a bridge of understanding between the Jews and Gentiles."

---

[1] The names of all the contemporary Polish Christians in this book have not been used for obvious reasons.

The earnestness of her plea, and the intensity of her own compassion for my people, moved me deeply. From the few sketches of her own background that she gave me during the course of our getting acquainted, I could not doubt her sincerity or the courageous character of her convictions.

By then, I was compelled to give serious thought to the combination of events. I was thinking, "Three times? Lord, is this a genuine call I should be heeding?"

I decided to try biblical Gideon's maneuver and throw out a fleece. I wrote to my Board requesting a leave of absence to make a trip to Poland, saying to myself, "If they grant it, I will consider the invitations I have received as God's providence." The immediate response from headquarters was affirmative.

We land late at Kennedy, and my connecting flight on Lufthansa to Frankfurt is barely possible to make. I am carrying two extra pieces of luggage filled with donated clothing for the people of Poland. A mix-up at the reservation desk, and I am sent here and there to get it straightened out. I feel like a refugee of old, caught in the bureaucracy of airport management. Huffing and puffing, I make it to the gate just in time, and we take off for the 7½-hour flight to Frankfurt, Germany. From there, I go to Warsaw.

Warsaw. I remember the last time I was there in the summer of 1945. I was 23 years old, all alone, and wandered on the streets that were full of rubble, not yet knowing the fate of my family. There were no Jews to be seen in the city where 350,000 Jews lived before the war. I could not have felt more forlorn that last time I was in Warsaw.

On May 11, 1986, I catch my first glimpse of the small airport at Warsaw as the plane breaks through the low cloud cover. A far cry from the dismal night train arrival so many years ago. Many people are waiting on the walkway built in front of the airport, an arrangement new to my experience. It resembles a type of bridge often seen over busy streets in the United States. The people wave and smile as they recognize deplaning friends and relatives.

The first clue that Poland is not as it once was presents itself in the form of two young, green-clad militia men waiting at the bottom of the ramp steps descending from the Lufthansa plane. We are lined up for passport inspection, and stand in line for customs and money-changing. The holiday-dressed Polish people arriving with me are laden with huge square suitcases. I have never seen such monstrous pieces of luggage, which I assume are full of merchandise unattainable or too expensive to buy in Poland. I pass through customs with no questions asked, remembering, not too fondly, the many times I travelled with no identification papers, and the terror that the thin, bespectacled officer with two-star epaulettes on his uniformed shoulders might have struck in my heart in those days. My declaration is stamped now routinely, and all is "kosher."

I hail a porter in a yellow-ribboned cap, who fetched a buggy for me. The man is about 45 or 50 years of age, and eyes me with some uneasiness. It is then I notice that other people are also staring at me with a mixture of curiosity and some other kind of reaction I have provoked. I realize it is the sight of a Jew with a long, gray beard. There are very few Jews and no long beards left in Poland. The younger people in the airport had probably never seen a beard like mine, and possibly had never even met a Jew. The older ones who stared perhaps remembered the familiar sight when three and a half million Jews populated Poland. Inwardly, the curious eyes make me feel strangely out of place, as though I had passed through some time-warp and suddenly been deposited into a "future" generation where I make an anomalous appearance.

I follow alongside the porter as he pushes the cart full of my luggage toward the exit gate.

"I haven't been here for 40 years," I comment to him, as though I owed somebody an explanation.

"Why have you waited so long?"

"They killed my people, and I could not come back—too much hurt—I lost them all."

"My granny perished, too. She never came out of prison," the porter adds his own hurt.

Our eyes meet in silent recollection of those terrible times, and I am reminded that not only Jews, but hundreds of thousands of Poles also suffered and were killed by the Nazis. If I am to be on a busman's holiday here, a message to the churches is clear in my mind. Humanity is one piece under God's judgment and mercy—victims and survivors, the good and the evil. I will speak of forgiveness, reconciliation, hope, and resurrection, by the grace of God through our Lord and Savior, Yeshua the Messiah.

"How much for a good meal in a restaurant?" I ask the porter.

"Fifteen hundred zlotys." (About $3.00 on the free market).

I pay him 500 zlotys, and look around for my welcoming party. They are close at hand, and greet me warmly. Sister S., my hostess during this visit, has brought two young people with her, an engaged couple who are involved in the Christian caring ministry.

"So you are here this time!" the motherly chaperone exclaims.

"What do you mean, 'this time?' You were expecting me some other time?"

"Yes, as a matter of fact, we were, and even came to the airport to retrieve you. We were told by your travel agent that you would arrive three weeks ago."

"Oi vey! Sorry about the misinformation, Sister S. I was unaware of the mix-up. I had my own troubles at the airport in New York, but I am definitely here now, and eager to hear what you have planned for my visit."

We pile into a small old car, which appears to be some type of Volkswagen. Mrs. S. asks for prayer before we drive away. The young man, I learn, has recently graduated from a school of theology, and is waiting for a pastorate. The four of us pray together, asking the Lord's blessing and protection.

The exhaust pipe is loose on the Volkswagen, and rattles loudly during the ride to a very old, five-story apartment house where the two women live. The outside stone walls are crumbling, and Mrs. S. explains that there have been no repairs on the building since before the war. We climb up dusty and well-worn wooden stairs to the ladies' apartment. Inside, the rooms are quite clean, the living-room walls are lined with books, and the pine board floor has been freshly waxed.

The pleasant warm surroundings relax me, and I suddenly feel the travel weariness. Sister S. suggests I take a hot bath and rest until tea time, and I am more than ready to do so. I know the next two and a half weeks are going to be exhausting and a sensory overload.

At tea later, I am informed that the young couple are taking me to a Jewish theater production that evening. The play is one by Isaac Bashevis Singer entitled, "Magician of Lublin." How can I tell these kind people that my brains are still somewhere over the Atlantic and I would rather spend a restful evening recovering from jet lag?

The theater is full of people and poorly ventilated. The air is dusty and our seats are in the upper last rows where it is extremely warm. I stay awake long enough to realize that the actors playing the Jewish roles are all Poles, and the dialogue is in Polish. With my experience of anti-Semitism in Poland, the idea of Poles playing Jews sets my teeth on edge. But of course my young companions know nothing of this, and so I keep it to myself. Fatigue overcomes me, and I doze through most of the two-act play.

The following day, Sunday, I am expected to give my testimony in a fifteen-minute talk at a Baptist church. My memories begin to stir—so many events—so long ago. What can I possibly say in fifteen minutes? No matter. My Polish is rusty, and I think I will be glad to sit down after that length of time has elapsed.

The young people return me to the apartment after the play, and I finally fall into bed about 11:00 p.m. The last thoughts I remember having before sleep comes are, "How shall I begin my testimony here in the land of my birth? Forty-seven years ago, I was a teen-ager who had no thought of ever leaving my beloved country . . . ."

Eliezer and Gentile classmate in front of the high school in Cieszyn

CHAPTER 2

Swastikas Overhead

At 5:00 a.m., I climbed into the makeshift elevator that creaked and groaned all the way to the top of the mill. Opening a window on the top floor, I scanned the bright morning sky. Not many people were yet stirring in the streets of the little town below, but smoke was coming from most chimneys, indicating that the day had begun in its households. As was customary in small communities, people were up with the sun to put in a long day at making a livelihood. Located a few miles from the Czechoslovakian border, my hometown, Skozcow, Poland, was an industrial city. Diverse factories produced hats, woolens (mainly uniforms and blankets for the Polish army), and bricks. There were also flour mills, a tannery, and a distillery. When the German army invaded Poland, the distillery was sabotaged by the Polish army, releasing thousands of liters of alcohol to run in the streets. The excited citizens swarmed after it with pots and pans, scooping up as much as possible in their utensils. The crazy booze bonanza was long remembered by those who lived to remember it.

I drew in a deep breath of the crisp autumn air. It was good to be alive and full of youthful strength and optimism. The political storm clouds which were gathering in Europe, particularly in neighboring Germany, were not intruding on my sense of well-being at that moment.

Suddenly, the wail of an air-raid siren pierced the peaceful scene. From the western sky came the roar of German war planes. I could see the swastikas on the tails of the planes as they thundered overhead. The Messerschmitts were on their way to Krakow and Warsaw with a lethal load of bombs. I stood in frozen disbelief as I watched the planes streak across the early morning sky and disappear into the horizon.

A black-out had been in effect for the past eight weeks in Skoczow. Soldiers were being called to duty. The second miller at Berman's flour mill, where I worked as a miller's apprentice, was now in uniform. Since the departure of the second miller, my work load had increased, although I still received the wages of an apprentice. My job was to fill sacks of grain and flour, and exchange flour for the grain brought to the mill. The transactions entailed carrying the 100-pound sacks on my back. It was hard work, but the strength it built into my lean, wiry body would soon prove to be a God-send.

The Nazis captured Skoczow the first day of the Blitzkrieg in Poland, September 1, 1939. Fast-moving German tanks cut through the unprepared Polish defense lines and rumbled into the tiny town nestled in the foothills of the Carpathian mountains. There had been no declaration of war. The German attack was so swift and sudden from an unexpected direction, the Poles had no chance to carry out their defense plans. Although the Poles fought stubbornly, they were no match for the mechanized German army.

I ran back to the old elevator and returned it to the ground floor of the mill. It had never seemed so slow before now. I darted through the empty streets toward our home at the crossroads, where my family operated an inn and restaurant. Before reaching the inn, I met two of my Gentile classmates, also running, but in the opposite direction.

"Come on, Eliezer!" shouted my tall friend, Franciszek

Kubaczka. "Let's get out of the city!"

Franciszek was a dark-haired, athletic figure of budding manhood. During the week, he worked as an apprentice in a lithograph shop, and on the weekend, he was a popular player on Skoczow's soccer team. Franciszek beckoned wildly to me with a sweep of his arm. It was a familiar gesture as we boys had been in tight spots together before, but Franciszek was not grinning with mischievous pleasure this time.

Wide-eyed and breathless at Franciszek's side was my jolly friend, Jozef Pieter, a blond-headed, stocky youth of seventeen. Jozef was the son of a well-to-do builder, and his family belonged to the intelligentsia of Skoczow. The three of us had been friends since childhood, and had shared many escapades together. Like the proverbial three musketeers, we were inseparable companions, and each one of us possessed a spirit of adventure which led to activities executed on the spur of the moment. Slightly older than myself and Jozef, Franciszek was usually the instigator of our adventures. The local notoriety we achieved was sometimes an embarrassment to the Urbach family, but my father never punished me for my participation in adolescent mischief. The elderly gentleman had neither the heart nor the strength to discipline his high-spirited teen-age son.

In the excitement of the present moment, Franciszek's leading was unquestioned. I stopped in my tracks, listened to the whine of artillery shells coming from the west, and with hardly a second thought, joined my friends in the flight from the city.

"This is . . . unbelievable," Jozef panted. "Where is the . . . Polish army? Where . . . are we running to?"

"Save your breath, Jozef!" Franciszek called back to the trailing musketeer. "This is no time to ask questions! Just keep up with us!"

The Polish army was in full retreat as the Germans pushed rapidly toward the city from the Czechoslovakian border. The only place the fleeing Poles managed to sabotage was the distillery. While the other factories in Skoczow were more valuable to the occupying German soldiers, blowing up the distillery at least destroyed the enemy's immediate access to unlimited alcoholic spirits to celebrate the first-run victory.

Unaware of my detour away from home, my parents, Heiman and Berta Urbach, younger brother Ernest, and Helena, our childhood nanny, gathered in the family's living quarters attached to the inn. Other members of our extended family household could be heard clattering furiously around in another part of the house. My maternal grandparents, and an unmarried aunt, younger sister of my mother, had come to live with us shortly after I was born. Only my old father would appear calm amidst the panic. In his eighty years, he had seen much trouble come and go.

As the first-born son in a large family of twelve children, ten of whom were step-brothers and sisters, Heiman Urbach bore the hatred of a step-mother who favored her own children by his father. During one of their frequent altercations, Heiman's step-mother split the boy's forehead with a chamber pot, which left a prominent scar. Soon thereafter, the 14-year-old ran away from home. He waited tables in a restaurant in Krakow until he was drafted into the Austrian army. All through his military service, Heiman kept the one hundred gulden he had saved from his restaurant work, hidden beneath his shirt in a secret pouch. After his discharge from the army, a matchmaker found him a wife, and with his savings, he first bought the restaurant in Skoczow. As he prospered, Heiman purchased the surrounding farm land, a flour mill, and a coal storage business. His first wife died after World War I, and his children with her were grown and married. Berta, my mother, was also a matchmaker's find, and was a woman half my father's age when he married her. She had given him two sons to his old age, myself and Ernest.

Due to the discrepancy in my parents' age, my maternal grandfather was younger than my father by several years. Papa commissioned his father-in-law to be tutor and disciplinarian for his young sons. A restless character even then, I found it hard to sit still for the long Hebrew and Torah lessons, and aggravated Grandfather to administer sharp blows across my knuckles for constant finger fidgeting.

At age ten years, one particular day was etched into my memory. Tiring of the lesson period, I began my usual distractions.

"Eliezer, you are not paying attention!" Grandfather admonished. "How will you grow up to be a godly Jewish man if you do not learn your Torah lessons? You will please stop drumming your fingers on the table!"

"Grandpa, I **am** listening," I protested lamely.

"Then keep your hands quiet! Now let us continue the lesson with no further interruptions."

"The lessons are dull, Grandpa, and I don't care about them at all!" I retorted in an outburst of resentment.

The remark angered Grandfather Fabiszkiewicz.

"You will not be insolent to your grandfather!"

A stout whack of his clenched fist crumpled my small hand against the tabletop, tearing off the middle fingernail. Grandfather poured kerosene over the bleeding finger as a disinfectant. The fingernail was permanently deformed, a fixed testimony to my childhood Torah lessons. The incident also ended Grandfather Fabiszkiewicz's role as tutor.

Several months later, I answered a knock at the door. Standing on the threshold was a tall, bearded man with side curls. He wore a long black coat, and a black hat. The man smelled of garlic, tobacco snuff, and sweat. As the first whiff reached my nose, I drew back in self-defense.

"Who are you?" I asked apprehensively.

"I have been hired by your father to teach you Talmud and Hebrew," the man answered in bad Polish. "I am your new melamed."

I was aghast at the prospect. The man's appearance was foreboding, and on top of the offensive body odors, he did not even speak good Polish. I wondered where Papa could have found him. The teacher was obviously imported from somewhere else.

"Do I have a choice?" I inquired in my most surly tone of voice, hoping to incline the stranger to reconsider this assignment.

"Your father did not say so to me," Mr. Mendelowitz replied coldly. "May I come in, please?"

I retreated a few steps back to allow my new teacher entrance into the house.

"Now, young man, where will we sit for your lessons?"

"Over there at the table, I guess." My hostility did not seem to intimidate him in the least.

"Your father wants you to be well-instructed for your Bar Mitzvah, and a Jewish education is hard to get these days. You should thank your Papa for providing one for you," Mr. Mendelowitz went on, ignoring my attitude. "Sit down, please."

The melamed put on his spectacles, and began the first instruction. Reading from his book in a dry tone, he rarely glanced up at my scowling face. The ordeal only added insult to injury, in the interest of Jewish training.

When my father came home, I pleaded with him.

"I can't do it, Papa! Mr. Mendelowitz smells awful, and I don't like him a bit. **Please**, Papa, one lesson is enough from him!"

"Very well, my son, in that case, we'll try another teacher. Your Bar Mitzvah is approaching. You must be prepared for it somehow."

Soon, a Mr. Battist arrived to continue my instructions. He was a small man, with grayish hair, and clean-shaven. Mr. Battist lived in Skoczow, and the new teacher made his living by trading in used sacks. Although his clothes frequently were dusted with flour, he was otherwise clean and pleasant. Mr. Battist was a scholar in modern Hebrew and English. Both languages intrigued me for non-academic reasons (I was a show-off at school and my aptitude for languages was a vehicle for impressing my provincial classmates).

The lessons went on for about a year. When I began to neglect doing my homework regularly, Mr. Battist reluctantly terminated the sessions. He bade farewell with a kindly reproach for failing to apply myself seriously.

"I cannot make you learn, Eliezer. Unless you study and learn for yourself, my time with you is in vain."

"I know, Mr. Battist," I admitted. "I'm sorry to disappoint you, but I will remember much that I have learned from you, believe me."

And it was so. Many years later, when I went to live in Palestine, I learned to speak Hebrew easily, and even more years later, English became another quickly-adopted language.

ॐ

When the German bombs began to fall, Mama and Helena tried to organize a hasty salvage plan. Ernest shadowed his father as Papa moved from window to window, searching the street. My younger brother was not endowed with the same reckless, adventuresome spirit that I had, and chose to follow placidly in his father's footsteps. Ernest was a serious-minded boy, wrapped securely in tradition and his own talent for mental order and careful planning. Spontaneity was not a natural personality trait, and the pros and cons of his activities were thoroughly calculated. Ernest was barely fifteen years old.

"Where is Eliezer? Why isn't he here yet?" Mama asked anxiously. "Where can he be? The mill is not a safe place, is it, Heiman?"

Papa did not want to betray the depth of his own concern for his eldest son, which would only intensify the panic of the women. With a steady voice, he replied.

"Eliezer is all right, Mama. The boy has good sense. He will take shelter wherever he is. Don't worry. We will see him soon. In the meantime, do what you think is necessary in case we have to leave our house temporarily. I will watch for Eliezer."

Hardly mollified by the tenuous reassurance of my good sense, Mama continued to move around the room distractedly, gathering up the items she treasured and hoped to save from looting or destruction.

"Lord, preserve us!" she muttered. "Must there always be trouble? Why can't we ever live in peace? What are we to do now? What to take? What to leave?"

The task of sorting out valued personal possessions under such stress was impossible. An exploding artillery shell which took off the chimney of the inn, mobilized Mama's practical sense, and she quickly began to pack provisions for the family and other people.

Jews did not prosper in Poland with any great ease. The Urbachs had been quite fortunate, and expressed their gratitude to God in wide generosity to those in need. The family was well-known for sharing their material benefits in the community. Both Heiman and Berta had earned the respect of their fellow citizens, and the only anti-Semitic attacks they experienced came through the peasants who drank heavily at the crossroads inn. When payment was asked for goods, some of these customers responded with curses. Most innkeepers were in no position to stop extending credit to the peasants. In this potato and rye country of large nobility-owned farms, the surplus crops were used to make whiskey. To market their product, the landlords built inns at the crossroads and usually rented them to Jews. The Jewish operators were especially vulnerable to abuse from drunken Gentile patrons. Heiman Urbach was an exception in that he had owned his inn for many years and was at liberty to expel offensive people. As far as I know, he did so only once, when he was much younger.

A band of gypsies invaded the inn and refused to leave for several days. Papa's regular business dropped off because customers refused to mingle with such rough company. The gypsies ignored Papa's reasonable requests that they depart the premises. At last, his patience came to an end. Papa appeared on the stairway wielding his World War I military sabre. He leapt upon a table, shouting in anger, "Get out! Get out! All of you! Get off my property at once!"

The gypsy rogues were thoroughly intimidated by the ferocity of Papa's command, and obeyed. Coarse insults Papa chose to ignore through the years, but he would not allow his business to be ruined.

It was during my three years of commuting from home to attend high school in Cieszyn that I saw tragedy looming for the Polish Jews. Waves of anti-Semitism had struck terror in Poland. Premier Jozef Pilsudski had a Jewish wife, and as long as he lived, he provided some protection for Poland's three and one-half million Jews. But after Pilsudski's death in 1935, Jew-hate increased under the influence of Germany's Adolf Hitler. Poland had the highest percentage of Jews of any European country, the Jews comprising ten percent of the Polish population. Between the two World Wars, the Jews were restricted in their economic, political, and educational rights.

Following Hitler's rise to power, Jews in positions of authority in Poland were systematically ousted. A Jew could no longer become a doctor, or enter officers' training school. In Cieszyn, I saw Jews beaten on their way to synagogue, and old Jewish men pulled by their beards, harassed and insulted by college students, all in the name of nationalism. Windows in Jewish shops were shattered. Anti-Semitic posters on the walls of public buildings read: "Jews go to Palestine!" and "Jew Communists get out!"

Another kind of propaganda had a medieval cast. Poles and Germans accused the Jews of living off the fat of the land, and of using others to work for them in shady enterprises. Jews were labeled as community parasites. Although I was the child of well-to-do parents who had attained their good position by legitimate hard work, I absorbed the prejudice against my people, and became sensitized to the accusations. Crushed and angry at such unjustified insults and attacks, I dropped out of school and returned home to work as an apprentice in Berman's flour mill. The townspeople of Skoczow knew that Eliezer Urbach did not have to do manual labor. In a naive way, I was trying to prove something, but could not articulate it to my prospective employer.

"So why do you want to work for me?" Mr. Berman, the Jewish owner, wanted to know, when I applied at his office.

"I'm tired of just going to school," I told him superficially. "I want to do something else for a change. Do you have a job for me?"

"Yes, I certainly could use some help right now. I'll soon lose my second miller to the army. You can start at once—tomorrow morning, in fact. Be here at five o'clock."

Mr. Berman appreciated having an industrious young worker at the mill, and he treated me as kindly as his disposition would allow. Although he was a good-hearted man, the burden of a grotesque physical appearance had shortened Berman's temper. His two ostanding features were a goiter and a large paunch.

Nevertheless, I liked my job at the mill. I enjoyed the heavy physical work, but more important, I felt that it nullified the sinister, anti-Semitic notions that I had been exposed to in Cieszyn. Earning an honest living by the sweat of my brow seemed to put me on an equal footing with other working people. No one could call me a Jewish "parasite" now. I did not relish being despised just because I was Jewish. It was my innocent belief that somehow my working would counteract the growing antagonism toward Jews in the community, as well as improve my own sinking self-esteem.

Being the oldest son in a religious Jewish family, I had grown up in the synagogue; indeed, my father had helped organize the synagogue in Skoczow, and served twenty years as its president. Like all other Jewish men, I was obligated by tradition to contribute my presence to the minyan, the quorum of ten adult males necessary for public prayers, and had often accompanied Papa to the synagogue since my Bar Mitzvah, (yes, I satisfied the requirements in time).

However, my Jewishness did not mean much to me. It represented a way of life, a way of thinking and doing certain things, a peculiar mentality. At the age of sixteen, I stopped saying prayers, wearing phylacteries—the leather religious accoutrements worn on the left arm and forehead—and attending synagogue. I also violated kashrut, the Jewish dietary laws. I found these customs irrelevant to my life, and a hindrance to my friendship with Gentiles. My parents were lenient, and did not pressure me for such disobedience. It was not too unusual for Jewish boys to rebel against tradition during adolescence. Rebellion began to take a dangerous turn as the political climate grew more threatening.

"We're going over the border again tonight, Eliezer," whispered Skiba, a mop-haired friend and **Sila** comrade. "Meet us at the usual place."

"All right—see you there at 5:00 o'clock," I answered in an aura of secrecy.

"Don't be late or we go without you," Skiba added. "Timing is important these days."

"I know, Skiba. We have to be more careful every time. You can count on me to be there."

In further search of a respectable identity, I joined a socialist workers' organization. At this stage of life, radical ideas attracted me. **Sila**, which meant, "strength" or "power," was a sports and social group for young people. Although the Communist party was outlawed in Poland in the early 1930's, **Sila** had former members of the Communist party among its ranks, and several other Jewish boys had joined. Many Communists had been sent to prison and severely beaten. As we watched these political victims return from punishment still zealous for their cause, we viewed them as contemporary heroes. Along with several other **Sila** members, I secretly stashed a red flag under my shirt while enroute to meetings and demonstrations just over the border in

Czechoslovakia. It was all very dangerous and exciting to a seventeen-year-old "revolutionary" idealist.

Four of us from **Sila** one evening boarded the 5:15 train to Cieszyn, Czechoslovakia. The workers' rally began with a march to the townsquare, where music, speeches, and red flag-waving created an atmosphere of impending political upheaval. The workers, mostly coal miners, were protesting hazardous working conditions, poor pay, and hunger. We Skoczow youths found the movement exhilerating, and nobly conspired by courageous, down-trodden people.

Suddenly, several squads of helmeted riot police on horseback rode into the square. Some of the police swung clubs and sabres, others fired tear gas bombs into the crowd, and still others manned water cannons.

"Run for it!" Skiba yelled. "Head for the train station!"

In the commotion and panic-striken crowd, we all became separated. I had relatives on the Czech side of Cieszyn, and fled to their home.

"Why, Eliezer, how nice of you to come to see us!" Aunt Helena greeted me unsuspectingly.

"Yeah, well, I thought I would get away from Skoczow for a little while," I replied nonchalantly, "and my mum has been wondering how you all are."

I stayed two days at my aunt's house before returning home, thinking over this latest escapade and being grateful that I had not been caught and involved my family in serious trouble.

"Where have you been, son?" Mama asked with a mixture of anxiety and exasperation in her voice. "Why do you just disappear for two days?"

"I just went to visit Aunt Helena, that's all." The half-truth was the best I could do. "She sends her regards, and said to tell you it is time for you to come over for a visit, too."

"Oh, Eliezer! Will you ever settle down? Now go wash for supper. I'm glad you visited your Auntie, but please don't leave town again without telling us. There is too much trouble brewing!"

❧

Now, as the sirens wailed and the Nazi planes rumbled overhead, my first reaction was a sense of excitement. I followed my companions instinctively. We had always stuck together in emergencies of our own making. But as I ran along with them, suddenly the stark realities of this situation struck me. This was no adolescent frolic. We were running for our lives. My free and peaceful life, stable home, and steady job had just been wiped out.

The three of us finally ran out of breath, and we stopped to rest in the stairwell of a shop. As we sat there puffing and heaving, the sirens ceased, and in a few moments, pandemonium erupted all around us. During the lull between the retreat of the Polish army and the arrival of the German front, the highway that ran through Skoczow became clogged with hundreds of refugees from the west, who were just five or six hours ahead of the advancing Germans. The citizens of Skoczow were inundated by the multitude who came on foot, horseback, or in carts, and burdened with all the personal belongings, clothing, and food that they could gather up before leaving their homes. It was a scene of utter confusion and panic.

When we had recovered our breath and collected our wits, it was time to make a plan. Realizing our different circumstances, I broke the silence.

"It looks like we had better part company here. I have a feeling the Germans will be sorting us Jews out now. You can go home safely. I think I'll keep going east."

"Nonsense!" Franciszek objected. "We're not splitting up. We're going with you!"

"But why do you two want to leave Skoczow? You are Gentiles and have nothing to fear from the Germans. For me, it's a different story. I don't know where to go, and it wouldn't be healthy for you to be traveling with a Jew now."

"It isn't going to be healthy for anyone as long as the

Germans occupy Poland," Jozef said. "What future do we have here now? Just look around us . . . our country is being ruined!"

"Jozef's right, Eliezer," Franciszek concurred. "A Pole is a Pole, and a German is a German. We'll take our chances with you in the east, if you don't mind."

I was in no mood to argue with my friends, and in my heart, I was grateful for their company. On one hand, I felt as dreary as the cold drizzle that had begun to fall. But, on the other hand, I was terribly excited at the adventure before us.

"All right then. Let's head for Przemysl."

"Good idea!" Franciszek agreed. "Przemysl it is!"

Russian troops invaded Poland on September 17, 1939, and occupied the eastern half of the country. The German army quickly seized control of the industrial and mining regions of southern Poland, and moved eastward. After only four weeks, the Poles succumbed to Hitler's forces. For the fourth time in its history, Poland was partitioned, this time into eastern and western sections, between Russia and Germany. The two conquerors signed a pact on September 28, splitting the nation. Many Jews, fearing the Germans more than the Russians, sought refuge in eastern Poland. However, it was not long before German tanks and marching columns overtook the streams of refugees at Jaroslaw, several miles from the German-Russian border. The Germans ordered the people to return to their homes. Unaware of this situation, we continued to make our way to the border town of Przemysl.

The first leg of our journey was a nearly 70-kilometer trip to Krakow. For three days, we traveled by train and on foot among thousands of other Jewish and Polish refugees laden with an infinite variety of crates, sacks, baskets, and rope-bound bundles of clothing and bread. Air raid sirens blew constantly, and all the towns along the route were blacked out. As the cargo train loaded with refugees approached the border, German planes attacked. The three of us had been on the train for several hours, and we were just gathering up our belongings in anticipation of detraining soon.

"The train has been hit!" Franciszek shouted. "It's stopping! Jump! Jump!"

When the disabled train came to a halt, we leaped out to the ground, ran through a potato field and into a small village. We stayed there for a week or more, hiding in barns and stealing food from the village markets and fields. Meanwhile, the German occupying forces arrived in the town, and began to round up refugees without identification papers.

Seeing their food supply in jeopardy, not only from the Germans, but from scavengers like three hungry boys from Skoczow, some villagers confronted us and strongly advised us to leave.

"You are in great danger here," one of the local farmers told us. "The Germans will get you sooner or later, and without safe conduct papers, you will be sent to a concentration camp or shot. The Germans are issuing papers to refugees at Jaroslaw, which permit them to return to their homes safely. You would be wise to go to Jaroslaw and obtain those papers. Otherwise, you may never see your homes and families again. Furthermore, we are not going to permit you to raid our food supplies any longer!"

The other members of the village delegation gestured emphatically in agreement.

We were not foolhardy. There was no choice, and we would be lucky to get to Jaroslaw for the needed papers before being picked up by the German military police. Carefully avoiding the uniformed threat, we slipped aboard a train for the border town, and maintained a position in the tightest crowd pack to stay out of sight.

"If my father knew where I am right now, he would be wild," Jozef remarked. "His son—a refugee hiding on a train for Jaroslaw! If we get home all right, I'll have some explaining to do."

"My father wouldn't be too surprised at anything I do any

more," Franciszek laughed nervously. "He gave up on me long ago!"

Although I did not communicate much with my father, the age gap being unusually wide between us, I knew that Papa had not "given up" on his son. I never interpreted his indulgence as indifference, and I respected my father for his character and dignity. The bond between a father and his eldest son in Orthodox Jewish families is particularly strong. Tradition dictates many mutual responsibilities, most of which I had turned over, exercising my "right" to do so very early. Now I reflected on the paternal patience in my home before adding a comment.

"My father probably wouldn't do much. He would just say a prayer that I was home safe. Whatever else he thinks, he keeps pretty much to himself, but he really doesn't have to tell me. Our religion spells out the rules of conduct, and I know what he expects of me. I know I've disappointed him a lot. I doubt if you two fellows understand how much. Christians seem to have more freedom than religious Jewish families, but then maybe I don't understand that either."

"Hush up, Eliezer!" Franciszek ordered. "Your being a Jew has never made any difference to us. Hey! The train is coming to a stop. We must be in Jaroslaw."

The passengers did not have to decide where to go. Parallel lines of German police channeled the refugees from each car to a large, gray concrete building near the station, where long queues of people waited their turns to be interrogated by officials. When our time finally came after several hours of standing in line, we were asked our name, age, address, nationality, and race.

"What do you mean—race, sir?" I asked politely.

"Are you Jew or Gentile?" the official explained gruffly.

"I am Jewish, sir."

A stamp of a different color went on my papers, imprinting a "J" in the appropriate square.

"You will return immediately to your homes. Here are your safe conduct papers. If you follow these orders, you will have no trouble. Be on your way now!"

Franciszek, Jozef, and I threaded our way back to the train station. Our sense of excitement was considerably dampened by now.

"Well," I remarked dryly, "my being a Jew may not make any difference to you, but it obviously does to the Germans. You are a blue 'G' and I am a red 'J.' "

"Oh, forget it, Eliezer," Jozef reassured me. "You got the same papers we did. Let's go home!"

Intermittently walking and riding the train as we had come, we retraced our journey. Jozef and Franciszek, who still did not seriously consider their lives in jeopardy, attached themselves to some girls along the way, but my thoughts now were all concentrated on my family and home. How were the Nazis treating my people? What I had already seen and heard gave me no cause for optimism. I grew impatient with the casual dallying of my friends, as if they were on another lark. Yet I could hardly blame them and kept quiet. As Gentile Poles, they believed that their lives would only be inconvenienced, at worst, stymied, for a while. They expected no lethal trouble from the Germans. But even at this early stage of the war, I had a premonition that something much worse was in store for the Jews. The red letter on the paper in my pocket made me feel uneasy. Three weeks after I had left home, I arrived at 218 Bielska Street, Skoczow, district Cieszyn, now officially annexed to Germany.

The sight of German soldiers and tanks stationed throughout the town was so sickening, I was already weeping before I reached the inn.

"Papa! Papa! Let me in—it's Eliezer!" I shouted as I pounded on the door.

The door was unlatched immediately, and I fell into my old father's arms.

"What have they done, Papa?" I cried out, totally distraught. "Where's Mama? And Ernest?"

With tears of relief blinding his age-worn eyes, Papa

clutched me by the shoulders and drew me into the house. Although I was appallingly dirty and infested with lice, Papa saw that I was well and unharmed. Mama came running from the kitchen when she heard my high-pitched voice. She gasped at the sight of me, but breathed a prayer of thanksgiving and embraced me, dirt, lice, and all. Recovering his composure, and seeing that I was alive and well, Papa began to answer my questions without yet asking where I had been for three weeks.

"The Nazis have taken away our license to sell food, drink, and lodging. They have also taken away our fields. They have stripped us of everything. Grandfather Fabiszkiewicz has been helping us to survive."

"Go on, go on," I urged. "Tell me everything!"

"Your grandfather is still able to make shoes as before. His customers are being allowed to come, but they are paying him in food now, and he has shared his provisions with us. Food is requisitioned from the producers by the Germans, and rationed to Polish citizens. The Jews receive the most meager quantities. The Germans, of course, receive full rations, the Poles, half rations, and the Jews, a quarter ration. The German military force has taken control of the police, local government, and the factories in Skoczow, and have issued occupation currency since our money is now worthless. Most of the townspeople have tried to appease the Nazis by identifying with them. Even my old friend, Motyczka, the barber, wears a swastika on his lapel in order to keep his job. I suppose we can't blame them. Everyone tries to survive somehow."

Papa sighed heavily as he went on speaking from the perspective of his long life. There comes a time when the pages of history become dull with repetition.

"Why must we suffer the repeated rise of barbarous social humanisms that keep civilization in jeopardy? There is always some pernicious political plague being spread by a maniac messiah which results in the destruction of millions of innocent people in the name of human progress. What kind of progress is this? It seems to me that most of the time, the world is engaged in survival against dark savage forces. When the real Messiah comes, he will put an end to all this evil. Our Scriptures tell us so."

Even after I told my parents about my own experience, the magnitude of the Nazi-bred calamity for the Jews was not then conceivable, although clues multiplied rapidly. Every day, new and more harsh demands were made by the Germans. Just a few days after I returned home, a work order was posted throughout the town. It read:

ORDER

All able-bodied Jewish men from the age of fourteen to sixty are obliged to work in places instructed by the Employment Exchange. People failing to comply with the order will be shot.

City Commandant

Approximately one hundred Jewish males reported to the Employment Exchange, headquartered in the town hall building. The Jews were put to work filling in the trenches and shelters made by the Polish army before the outbreak of the war. With picks and shovels, and loads of stone, the men were forced to work long hours at manual labor without pay. Nazi guards, armed with pistols and machine guns, kept the commandeered workers under close surveillance. I was aware that the work was mainly a means of suppression and humiliation. After two weeks of hard labor under the Nazis, I began to plot a second escape. A quiet oppressive atmosphere of doom pervaded the city. Life was ebbing out of the Jewish community. But what was to be done about my family? Mercifully, my father answered that question himself.

Sitting in his old reading chair one evening, Papa beckoned for me to come near to him. Mama knew that some prearranged time had come. She moved behind Papa's chair and gripped the back of it. She was dressed as usual in a housedress covered by a full-length apron, and with her hair pulled back into a bun, she was a picture of traditional Polish womanhood. Crying softly, she waited for Papa to speak.

"Poland is lost and will not be a fit place for you to live, Eliezer. It is doubtful if Jews will be permitted to live at all. Hitler is a fanatic Jew-hater, and it appears that he intends to crush us under his boot. Who knows how far he will go to satisfy his monstrous vendetta against us? Do you understand what I am saying?"

I tried to absorb my father's words. Above my head hung the single ceiling lamp. From it dangled fly paper which rotated erratically when the air was disturbed, casting strange reflections on the light-colored walls and on the immaculately scrubbed pine floor. It seemed to me that the whole world had suddenly spun out of its orbit, and I felt dizzy.

"Yes, Papa, I know. The future is bleak for us," I replied numbly.

A moment of silent communication passed between father and son. I sensed what his next words would be.

"You must go, my son, and save your life," Papa said resolutely.

Mama caught her breath, and put her hand over her mouth to stifle her sobs. Her world, too, was crumbling.

"But what about Ernest?" I responded quickly. "He must leave, too! And you, and Mama, and all of us!"

"No," Papa went on. "Ernest has made his own decision. He is going to stay here with us for the time being. He is doing well in his trade school, and is convinced that our situation is only temporary. He is sure that the free world countries, most surely the United States of America, will come swiftly to end this Nazi terror. He has hope for the future here. We have considered his wish to remain in Skoczow for now. Ernest is still very young, and if Allies come soon to divert Hitler, he may escape the worst of it. Also, as you know, your brother is cautious by nature, and the times call for great risk-taking. You are better equipped for that. I think it is best that you go alone."

To the best of his ability, Heiman Urbach was trying to insure the survival of both his sons, according to their respective strengths and abilities. Not until I had a son of my own did I fully realize how difficult and painful Papa's choices must have been, which he knew may have assigned life or death to us.

I swallowed past the large lump in my throat, fought back the tears, and once more bravely entreated him.

"We will all go, Papa, the whole family! Come, let's pack our belongings! Why not all of us?"

But even as I protested, I already knew what the family's decision was, and Papa immediately confirmed it.

"No, we will stay. Your mother and I have already discussed it thoroughly. Do not make things more difficult for us. You are our hope for the future and, Lord willing, you will live to fulfill it. Go, my son, and may God protect you."

Heiman Urbach arose from his chair and did what might have been expected from the white-haired Jew who had kept the traditions of his people all of his life. With reverent dignity, he placed his hands upon his eldest son's head and pronounced the blessing given to Israel's sons thirty-three centuries before:

> "The Lord bless you and keep you:
> The Lord make his face to shine upon you, and be gracious
>   to you:
> The Lord lift up his countenance upon you, and give you
>   peace."

As the patriarch of the Urbach family spoke the last words of the ancient Aaronic blessing over me in Hebrew, the fulfillment of the blessing was beyond my imagination at that moment. Any kind of peace seemed impossible.

"Quickly now, get your things together, and be gone," my father commanded, as he concealed his trembling hands behind his back.

Somberly obedient, I went to my room, and found Mama

and Helena already preparing a bundle of clothing and food for me. When they had finished, I strapped the provisions to my back, and the family gathered in the living room for the parting. Ernest had arrived home from his trade school, and was greatly dismayed when Papa explained what was happening in the household. The day of separation had finally come. We were a happy family, and we two brothers were quite spoiled. Ernest was not able to emulate my recklessness, nor rashly abandon the security of tradition, but despite the difference in our temperaments, we had a close relationship, and rarely quarrelled.

"I guess I'm ready to go," I said, with as much confidence as I could muster.

"Very well," Papa replied. "Be alert, and take care of yourself."

He then handed me a roll of bills. "Here are a thousand German marks. This should get you out of the country."

I was stunned at the amount of money Papa was offering me. I shook my head in a silent refusal to accept such a substantial sum.

"Take it!" Papa ordered. "We will soon have no use for it here, and it may buy freedom for you."

Reluctantly, I took the money and stuffed it inside my stockings and deep into my knee-high boots.

"Thank you, Papa. I'll never forget your generosity and love."

I felt the sharp pain of sudden maturity, and I had never felt so close to my father. We embraced each other with great emotion, both of us thinking it was for the last time.

My mother waited her turn to say goodbye. I threw my arms around her and planted a kiss on her forehead. Mama choked out a blessing, then added,

"I pray that God will bring you and your brother together again somewhere, sometime. Do be careful, Eliezer, and be healthy. You will be in all of our prayers constantly."

What else could a mother say? Grief threatened to break

through the thin-sounding words of farewell, but for my sake, Mama kept her anguish in check. She spared me from having to leave an hysterical mother.

Helena stood in the background, her heart throbbing with pain as she watched the Urbach family do their best to cope with a grievous situation. Helena was a Gentile and a Catholic, providential circumstances of birth which gave her reasonable immunity from political trouble in Poland. But she had been nanny to Ernest and me since we were born, and had taken considerable part in our upbringing. Having no family of her own, we were her surrogate children. Our fate was of great concern to her also. I went to her now.

"Thank you for everything, Helena. I'll always have good memories of your kindness. Do what you can for my parents, and watch over Ernest while I'm gone. Don't worry, I'll be back after the war."

Helena, a woman of imposing stature and long, comforting arms, encompassed me in her familiar strong embrace. No doubt, the many years of caring for this energetic, willful child of devout Jewish parents flashed through her mind as she spoke.

"May God speed you to safety, Eliezer. Remember, you take cold easily, so try to stay warm and dry. Many people will be coming and going through Skoczow, so we will hope to hear news of your whereabouts by some courier."

"Yes, Helena, of course! You will be hearing from me soon," I replied optimistically.

Helena released me and adjusted the pack on my back. I know now that her own sorrow was greatly mixed with anger. The lives of the family she had served for so long were being cruelly and inexplicably broken. We had done nothing to deserve this. Helena was wondering if the rest of the world knew or cared about what was going on here.

Turning at last to my brother, I grasped him strongly by the arms, and firmly vowed,

"I'll keep in touch if I can, Ernest. Stay well, and keep out of the Germans' way as much as possible. Who knows? You may be right about the war, and we'll all be together again soon."

I could see that Ernest was momentarily torn between his decision to remain with our parents, and wanting to go with me, but his own kind of optimism led him to keep the course he had elected to follow.

"Yes, I'm sure this trouble will end soon, and things will get back to normal. May your luck be all good, Eliezer." Ernest's voice broke before he finished, and he turned to hide the tears.

I pulled my cap over my head, buttoned my jacket, and looked around the room one last time, until my eyes came to rest upon the little group of people frozen together in traumatic sadness, and unable to speak more. My father stood like an old soldier, his erect posture communicating strength and courage to me, but his eyes were glistening. He was gripping Mama's hand tightly, and Helena had Ernest braced in her arm across his shoulders. I turned and strode out of the door in search of the elusive peace which had been bestowed upon me with the Aaronic blessing.

Once again, I was about to embark upon a journey with an unimaginable ending. I could not have fully guessed then that for the Jews, the German occupation of Poland would mean pogroms, collective fines, destruction of synagogues, arbitrary arrest and imprisonment, social ostracism, and endless humiliation. The Jews were a helpless minority in the midst of a murderous, overwhelming majority. Neither I, nor any of my people yet, envisaged the incomprehensible horror of Hitler's "final solution"—his barbarous attempt at a total physical annihilation of the Jews. Nor could I know that I would be one of the few to survive the Nazi Holocaust.

CHAPTER 3

Escape to a Communist "Haven"

Two other Gentile friends, who were more infected with the spirit of adventure than tragedy, decided to accompany me this time on the flight to freedom. We had discussed the plan earlier. Tadek Jurczynski, the bright son of a schoolmaster, and Antek Ferfecki, whose father was a civil engineer, abhorred the German occupation of our country, and rightly figured that their immediate future was questionable at best.

"They will never make me wear a swastika!" Tadek declared. "My father said he had no choice, if he wanted to keep his job at school to provide for the family. He told me it didn't mean that he was a Nazi, but under the circumstances, he had to wear their silly emblem. I don't know—maybe he is doing the right thing for Mama's sake and the rest of us. Still, I can't wear one of those things."

"Me neither," Antek joined in. "The Nazis have forced my father to work for them. They conscripted all the Polish engineers, but I'd rather die first."

"You just might do that, Antek," I warned my friends. "The Nazis mean terrible business. They won't tolerate your refusal to capitulate for long. They have ways to dispose of those who refuse to obey their orders."

"We know, but we still have a choice. We can go to Russia and wait out the war there. That's the best idea, and we'd better not stay around here too much longer. Let's go as soon as possible," Tadek urged.

I found these two companions quickly after leaving home. They were still eager to get out of German-occupied Poland and were already prepared to go. Together we set out on foot for the nearest large city, Krakow, approximately 70 kilometers northeast. No trains were available now since the retreating Polish army had demolished all the railway bridges. The highway, which had previously been a moving river of refugees, was now virtually empty, and we made our way without encountering any German soldiers. Yet, the very absence of traffic was unnatural, and gave us an eerie feeling. What had happened to our country and its people in just a few short weeks was almost beyond belief. The heavily merchanized Nazi "wehrmacht" (armed force) had quickly crushed all Polish resistance, and driven all the way eastward to the San River. Russia had taken eastern Poland with little opposition, "to protect its own frontier." Politically, the country of Poland no longer existed. The barren road mutely testified to its temporary disappearance as a political entity.

After several days of walking, we were foot-sore and tired when we reached Krakow, where we sought lodging in a convent which had opened its doors to displaced persons. A poor religious order even before the war, the convent's facilities were greatly over-taxed with the influx of refugees. The Catholic Sister who let us in sighed heavily at the sight of three more needy ones, but welcomed us sympathetically.

"As you can see, young men, we are already overcrowded. We have no sheets or blankets left to give you, but you may sleep on the floor on those straw mattresses over by the wall. I hope you will not be too uncomfortable."

"Thank you very much, Sister. We appreciate your hospitality, and the safe night's sleep," Tadek answered for all of us. "We'll be on our way at sunrise."

"Good luck, and God bless you. May He bring you safely to your destination. I will say a prayer for you." The nun smiled warmly, and began to thread her way slowly through the throng of people surrounding her. I was impressed with the nun's serenity amidst such chaos in the convent.

"She made us feel more like guests than refugees. Nice lady," I remarked, more to myself than to my companions, who seemed to take the hospitality for granted, even under the circumstances.

Early in the morning, we began the most dangerous part of our journey. As before, the immediate goal was Przemysl, a town on the German-Russian border. The San River divided the city itself, as well as the eastern and western sectors of occupied Poland. From Krakow eastward, the railroad tracks were intact, so we decided to take the train as far as Zoravica, which was still several hours walking distance from Przemysl. We thought a more cautious entrance into the border town was wise, and opted for detraining early.

Unlike the highway, the train was packed with people. Few Poles owned automobiles, and the common means of transportation were horse-drawn vehicles. Since the Germans has requisitioned all the horses, travel from town to town was limited to the railway lines.

No one was allowed to travel without the proper papers, and by now, no Jew could secure travel permits. For me, if caught, the penalty for such an attempt could be imprisonment or death. For my Gentile companions, the treatment would have been much less harsh.

Purchasing tickets was not a problem, but the presence of German soldiers who filled the station posed an imminent danger. Everyone in the station yard was eyed with suspicion. My heart pounded and my palms were damp with sweat as we awaited the train. Time seemed to stand still. Where was the train! Each time a soldier walked near, I did my best to look calm and unconcerned, while my companions chattered to themselves to keep from appearing too furtive. Somehow, we escaped questioning. Late that afternoon, the lumbering old train departed for Zoravica with us aboard.

It was a slow and tortuous ride, especially for me. The train ground to a halt at every little station, where German soldiers were on duty. At any moment, one of the guards might come down the aisle to inspect papers. Miraculously, only one such inspection fell upon us. Sitting next to the window, I made myself as small as possible and pulled my cap over my Jewish face. Tadek and Antek flanked me protectively in the next two seats toward the aisle.

A German in a grey-green uniform stopped in the narrow aisle and swayed over our seats.

"Papers, please!" he ordered sharply.

Tadek and Antek quickly handed over their identification papers, which the German examined carefully.

"Where are you going?"

"To western Przemysl," Tadek lied, "to visit my uncle there."

"And who is that?" the officer asked, pointing to me.

"He's asleep," Antek volunteered. "Not feeling well either, but he's all right. He's my brother. You don't have to wake him. His papers are in order, too. We all got them at the same time."

A shiver ran through my body under my jacket as I listened to the conversation. "Oh, God!" I thought, and then vaguely wondered if this first brush with certain disaster had elicited a prayer. For all of my rebelliousness against tradition, I had never used the name of God profanely. My Orthodox upbringing had kept me at least that respectful of Deity.

"Umpf!" the German solder snorted. "See that you stay out of trouble in Przemysl."

Our innocent act was convincing enough, and the documents were returned to their owners. The German had been lenient for some reason. Perhaps this particular young man was still hesitant to use his recently acquired power of life and death over a conquered people. Later in the war, an unidentified passenger certainly would not have been spared the routine inspection of papers as I was this time.

As the German soldier left our car, we breathed deeply in relief.

"That was a close one!" Tadek whistled through his teeth.

"Yeah, it sure was," I agreed. "Thanks a lot for the cover. You were lucky it worked. I hate to think what would have happened if the German had called your bluff. You were asking for big trouble on my account. I hope it doesn't happen again —the next German may be more into his work!"

"No thanks are due," Antek shrugged. "We enjoyed bluffing out that croaking German frog!"

It was well past midnight when the train arrived in Zoravica. Rain was falling hard, and the cold night air went through to the bone. Already tired and hungry, we had to walk four more miserable hours toward Przemysl. As we approached the city, the rain lessened, then mercifully stopped altogether, but we were soaked to the skin, and much too uncomfortable to appreciate the break in the weather.

Entering the western sector of Przemysl, we found a small cafe where we sought food.

"What do you have to eat here?" I inquired of the proprietor.

"Where did you come from? Don't you know there's a war going on?" the man said with dull sarcasm. "Food we don't have anymore. The menu is black bread and imitation coffee made from barley. No sugar, but we have boot-legged some saccharin."

"That's fine," Tadek responded. "Bring us what you have. We can pay for it."

We sat at a table, and the owner of the cafe shuffled off to fill the meager order. The nourishment was not much, but the coffee was warming and the bread stopped the hunger pangs for the time being.

"So far so good," Tadek summarized. "We're almost there. We just have to cross the border now, and it will soon be daylight so we can see where we are going."

Antek hardly felt refreshed, and he was having second thoughts about this adventure, but it was far too late to express his reservations. He merely nodded his head in agreement. I, of course, had no alternative. Concentration camp most certainly awaited me back in Skoczow. I finished gulping down the coffee and got up from the table, eager to press onward, hopefully to freedom.

"Let's go! Maybe the border guards are sleepy."

"Ha! We should be so lucky," Tadek chuckled nervously.

Back on the highway just before dawn, we headed for the bridge which crossed over to Russian-held Przemysl. As the bridge came into view, we quickened our pace with excitement. My mouth went dry, and I felt my heart thumping against my ribs. I had no identification papers, and there could be no tricks this time if I were caught. Trotting ahead of my friends, I suddenly stopped short. The road to freedom was blocked!

Menacing soldiers patrolled the bridge, Germans on one end and Russians on the other. I motioned toward a hilltop from which the river could be surveyed, and we climbed in silence. From this vantage point, we could see a large group of people trying to cross the river in boats and rafts. Our optimism mounted as we thought of joining this flotilla to freedom, but that hope was soon crushed.

"Look what's happening down there! Oh, no! God! Those poor people!" Antek's voice quavered as he watched the scene taking place below us.

Horsemen on the opposite bank intercepted the terrified people as soon as they landed on the shore, and herded them back into the boats. Using the butt end of their rifles, the border guards prodded the refugees roughly as though they were cattle. Mingled screams, yelling, and cursing rent the air.

"We certainly can't cross there," I glumly expressed the obvious. "Let's follow the river for a while and see what possibilities there might be further on."

The three of us wandered desolately along the river for several hours. That afternoon, we rested beneath a tree some distance upstream. Escape to the east had eluded us. As I sat watch on the grassy hillside overlooking the river, I thought about my home and all the terrible changes that had brought me to this precarious perch. My confidence in a successful end to this long journey was waning. While I gazed dejectedly at the meandering river which flowed along oblivious to our plight, suddenly, something bobbing on the water caught my attention. It was a boat tethered by a chain.

"Tadek! Antek!" I called out in a hoarse whisper. "It's a boat!"

"Where?"

"Down there! Look!"

"You're right! Shall we go down?" Tadek asked tentatively.

"Of course!" I was already leading the way.

Anticipating escape, we scrambled down the slope toward the river to make a closer inspection. The chain had no lock!

"That's a piece of luck! I can just lift the chain off its mooring post," I said as I tugged it loose.

"The boat is just the right size, too," Antek added, "like someone left it here for us."

"Quiet down!" Tadek ordered. "We don't want to spoil our luck."

Making sure no one was in sight, we clambered aboard the boat, pushed off, and silently rode the current, anxiously watching the banks for border guards. We were easy targets now, the only visible boat on the river in the immediate vicinity. In a short while, we touched the eastern shore about a mile downstream, and hastily grounded the little boat.

"Get down! Stay on your hands and knees! Head up the bank

and keep low in the bushes!" Tadek's crisp orders kept us moving cautiously.

On guard for horsemen, we crouched in the underbrush, listening intently for any sound. All was quiet. Nothing moved. We had reached the highway that followed alongside the course of the river. Directly in front of us was a large farmhouse.

"Do you think anyone is there?" Antek whispered. "Doesn't look like it from here."

"Let's be certain," I cautioned. "You know, the Germans have confiscated places like this and billeted soldiers in them. This is no time to take chances."

For an hour, we surveyed the house. At last, satisfied that no one was there, we were ready to move. Emerging into the open, we began to walk briskly along the highway.

"Hey! We made it!" Tadek leaped triumphantly in the air. "We're in Russian-occupied Poland! Can you believe it! Follow me, Comrades!" Antek made a mock salute and marched off behind our leader.

While my two exuberant friends were celebrating our successful escape, I was already thinking about our next problem, which was, where to go from here. Our destination in the eastern sector of Przemysl was the home of Tadek's uncle who was a high school music teacher there. But we had no idea where the road led, or which direction we should go on it.

The first people who came into view on the road were a group of Orthodox Jews, traveling in a horse-drawn cart. They were dressed in traditional long black coats and wore wide-brimmed black hats. Their side curls bobbed at the edge of their beards as the cart bumped along the rough road. I was surprised to see Jews traveling in the open and apparently free of concern. Catching up with the Jewish men, I spoke to them in Yiddish.

"Good day, gentlemen. Which way to Przemysl?"

"Straight ahead," one of the men answered. "Just keep going the way you are and you will come to it."

Out of curiosity and natural anxiety, I also inquired, "How

do the Jews fare in Russian territory?"

"The rich Jews have had trouble with the Ukrainians," the spokesman replied. "The Poles made tax-collectors of them in the past, and some became wealthy and unpopular. The common people and the religious are unmolested, as long as we keep quiet and stay out of radical politics. The Ukrainians blame us for Communism, and the Communists hate us because we won't assimilate. Politically, we cannot please anyone."

I thanked the Jews for the information, and the three of us continued on until we reached the town. A small bridge made a picturesque entrance into it, and two Russians in strange garb flanked the gateway. They wore peaked felt hats, long curly-napped coats, and carried elongated rifles attached with queer bayonets. The bayonets resembled the prong of a pitch fork rather than a blade. Although the guards presented a formidable sight, they were only bridge keepers, and paid no attention to us as we crossed over, feigning nonchalance while maintaining vigilant eyes on the guards.

Przemysl was a county seat town with a population of 20,000 or more, mostly Poles, Ukrainians, and Jews. It lay in a territory alternately known as Eastern Poland or the Western Ukraine, depending upon the tides of political sovereignty. Poland's powerful neighbors had a habit of dividing up the country, and at the present time, in 1939, there was no Poland at all.

Having entered the eastern sector of Przemysl, the next objective was to find Tadek's uncle who had resided there for many years.

"Where does your uncle live, Tadek?"

"I think we had better ask someone. I haven't been here by myself before, and I'm not familiar with the place. My uncle will be well-known though. Those children over there can probably tell us."

Tadek was right. The group of youngsters playing on the street provided directions, and we soon found the house. The dignified, grey-haired gentlemen was joyfully surprised when he opened the door to see the face of his favorite nephew.

"Tadek!" Mr. Jurczynski exclaimed. "Can I believe my eyes? What are you doing here? You look a sight! Come in, come in, all of you!"

"These are my friends from Skoczow, Uncle, Antek Ferfecki and Eliezer Urbach." Tadek introduced us. "We've had quite a time getting here."

"I can see you have," Mr. Jurczynski said. "You must tell me all about it."

Tadek did not have to tell his uncle that we were ravenously hungry. He ushered us immediately into the kitchen, and while the music teacher prepared something for us to eat, we told him the story of our flight from Skoczow.

"Unbelievable! Frightening! These are tragic times. What can we do?" Mr. Jurczynski interspersed reactions of horror between pauses in the conversation while we ate as though we were hollow to the toes.

"There is deprivation and oppression in eastern Przemysl, but nothing compared with the plight of the Jews under the Nazis. You must stay here and rest awhile. Eliezer, you are reasonably safe here for the present. I am so glad you have come. For you, the Russian bear is tamer than the German pig!"

For three days, we stayed with Tadek's uncle. It was time enough for me to collect my mind and to observe the surroundings. Now under the red flag of Russia, I had my first glimpse of the Communist "haven" we had come to. There were some stark differences from the socialism I had championed as a member of **Sila**. Victorious slogans and enthusiastic marches in Poland and Czechoslovakia gave way to endless bread lines of weary citizens standing for hours in the cold weather. During our stay in Przemysl, the three of us had to get up in the middle of the night in order to secure a place in the bread line when the bakery opened at 3:00 a.m. Rations were so small, we had to go through the line a number of times to obtain enough bread for all of us.

People wearing red stars, indicating Communist party membership, were in charge of keeping order in the bread lines, and supervising the flow of rations. The red star obviously conferred special privileges. A miserable patch of red cloth made a new "elite," and the common people still fared badly.

Not wanting to infringe upon the hospitality of Tadek's uncle too long, further plans had to be made. Mr. Jurczynski was very kind and insisted that we were welcome to stay, but we knew we were straining his resources.

"How would you like to go to Lvov?" I suggested. "It's about 75 miles east of here. We can go by train. I have an aunt living there. I don't know her very well, but I'm sure she will take us in. We have to leave here soon, and I don't have a better idea. What do you think?"

"Sounds all right to me," Tadek agreed. "What's to lose?"

"Lvov is a big city, and we might not be so conspicuous there. Good suggestion, Eliezer," Antek added his consent.

Lvov was one of the largest towns in the Russian-occupied territory, a manufacturing and trade center with a population of over 300,000. We happened to arrive during the celebration of the October Russian revolution. Huge Russian tanks and mobile weapons were parading through the streets. For a few minutes, we stood and watched a brigade of Russian soldiers pass by in their stiff marching formation. Polish and Russian troops had clashed many times in past history, and the repeated territorial disputes were often settled at the expense of Poland. The display of current Russian sovereignty stirred our Polish national pride, but we did not flirt with trouble by showing it.

"The blessing of Communism in review," I observed in a low voice to my friends. "Seems to me the only thing new about this social order is the uniform."

I was maturing rapidly. It was yet two months before my eighteenth birthday, but I had already had some heavy courses in recent political theory in the open classroom of life. Nazism, Communism, Fascism—what did it matter which label cloaked cruelty, violence, and oppression? The exploitation of the common people, the death-dealing policies, and idiotic propaganda campaigns were hardly distinguishable in the different totalitarian regimes. I wondered, how is it possible in the 20th century, in this so-called advanced stage of civilization, that tyranny and injustices are so wide-spread in the world? I suddenly remembered my father's oft-repeated hope for the human race. "When the Messiah comes . . ." Well, I thought sardonically, the Messiah is overdue.

Still suspicious of Russian benevolence toward Jews, I had written the address of my relatives on the palm of my hand rather than on paper. The writing could be obliterated quickly with a touch of some spittle. Leaving the crowds and commotion, we again asked our way to the house of my Aunt Emma, the widow of my much older step-brother. Emma had remarried long ago and moved away from Skoczow. I was born many years after this step-brother was grown and later killed in the first World War and so had little contact with the second family. Nevertheless, Emma welcomed her visitors, fed us well, and gave us a night's lodging. We departed early the next morning for the city of Stanislav, which we had decided was to be our final destination.

Now dependent upon my relatives for assistance, the next stop had to be Stanislav, about 110 miles southeast, where another step-sister lived, also named Emma. She and her family fled Skoczow just a day before the war started. The daughter of Papa's first wife, Emma was now about 55 years old. Her son-in-law was a successful physician in good standing with the Russian authorities. He secured Russian citizenship papers for Emma and her family, which protected them from being exiled to Siberia. Unfortunately, Russian citizenship did not protect them from the Germans. When Hitler invaded Russia, they were all killed by the Nazis.

The thousands of exiles and refugees displaced by the war were regarded as suspicious flotsam and jetsam floating on the

Russian landscape. All exiles were required by the Communist government to register themselves and their nationality. Noncitizens were routinely rounded up and told that they were being returned to their native countries. Instead, they were shipped off to Siberian labor camps.

Emma was full of concern for the family she had left in Skoczow.

"What is the news from Skoczow, Eliezer?" she asked anxiously. "How are the folks? Are they safe? What are the Nazis doing to the people there? We have heard terrible rumors that surely must be exaggerations."

"I'm not sure what is going on now, Aunt Emma. The three of us left some time ago. The situation was very bad already, especially for the Jews. The Nazis had taken over everything, including Papa's restaurant and fields. The family was barely surviving. On top of that, the Nazis were forcing the Jews to do stupid hard labor for no pay, and it looked like worse was to come. Papa and Mama insisted that I run for it. Ernest stayed home, hoping for a soon end to it all. That's all I can tell you."

I was choking out the words. It was painful to think about my home and family. But here I was in Stanislav, and second thoughts about my departure from Skoczow were useless now. It was Papa's last wish that I leave home. It was not helpful to wonder if I should have stayed anyway. What is done is done. For several years to come, I would be propelled through life and death situations by many such don't-look-back decisions.

As I slept securely the next few nights, it appeared that God's providence had brought me safely thus far, at least I knew that is what my parents and Helena would say about it. But where to next? I thought of my father's blessing, and wondered if I would ever find peace.

❧

While staying with Emma, we began to make some more long-range plans.

"The Romanian border is not too far from here," Tadek

opened with his idea. "I can make it alone without any trouble. There's no sense in your putting your head in a noose, Eliezer. I'll go scout the country, and find out how safe it is for you there. I'll be back soon."

"I'm going back home to Skoczow," Antek decided. "I want to know what the situation is with my family. If they are all right, and I can get out again, I'll bring some of your clothes back to Stanislav for you, Eliezer. I'll see your folks and find out how they are, too. The truth is, I'm homesick, and maybe I can find some way to help out our countrymen there."

"Well, good luck to you both," I said. "Don't be dead heroes. I want to see you again!"

"Don't worry, friend," Antek grinned. "We've proved to be slippery ones, right?"

"You know it!" Tadek rejoined. "Manage to take care of yourself while we're gone, and stay out of trouble until we get back, you hear?"

The next day, Tadek and Antek waved off and disappeared in opposite directions. I was sorry to see them go. They had been loyal friends for a long time, and I would miss them very much. I saw Tadek only once again. He returned from Romania with a good enough report, but another event occurred during his absence which changed my course. Tadek went back to Romania alone, and thence to England. Antek made one successful trip back to Stanislav with a suitcase full of my clothes as he had promised, but I was not at home when he arrived. He left the suitcase with Aunt Emma, and hurriedly left again without waiting to see me. Sometime thereafter, I learned that Antek had become involved in smuggling. He was caught and executed by the Nazis.

🦎

One afternoon, shortly after my good friends had left Stanislav on their respective missions, an urgent knocking came at the door. Emma opened the door to find Ernest standing there—dirty, disheveled, and trauma etched on his face.

"Eliezer! Come quickly!" Emma cried out. "Dear God! It's Ernest!"

Together we helped my weak, hungry brother into the kitchen, where Emma immediately began to prepare hot milk and bread.

"What has happened to you, Ernest?" I was beside myself to hear what my only brother was going to say.

Ernest began to tell us a horrifying story.

"Soon after you left home, Eliezer, the Germans issued another order for all Jewish men in Skoczow from 14 to 60 to assemble, on pain of death if we did not comply. They told us we were being relocated to work camps. We were taken to the train station and packed into cargo cars. There was hardly room to move. For two days we traveled like that, with no relief. When we reached Krakow, our train was combined with a larger one, loaded with still more Jews. We were transported to the San River where the guards threw open the doors and began yelling, 'Out! Out!' We were stiff and weak from our confinement, and not moving fast enough to please them. To hurry us up, the soldiers began firing their weapons into the air. Panic broke out, and everyone started to run. Then the Germans began to fire directly on us. They machine-gunned hundreds to death on the spot. Somehow, I managed to escape and get across the river. Most were not so lucky."

Ernest was sobbing uncontrollably as he finished his story. Aunt Emma and I sat in stunned silence. Nazi brutality was incomprehensible.

When Ernest had recovered somewhat from his ordeal, he and I enrolled in a college which had been established by the Russians to train teachers for their newly-occupied territory. I also worked part-time as a cashier at the school to support us. Food was scarce and expensive. I enjoyed the pedagogical school and did well. Classes were taught in Ukrainian, a language I learned quickly.

However, the students soon discovered that the courses

were taught from the Communist point of view. Many historical facts were distorted, and the instructors brooked no dissent from the curriculum. The Polish students became alarmed after a young Pole, by the name of Janek, dared to mock the claim that Russians had invented the radio and airplane. Thereafter, Janek was seen no more. Other people, for less obvious reasons, also began to disappear. Policemen, government employees, priests, teachers, large property owners, army officers and their families, all were particularly subject to removal by the Communist regime. We heard that people were rudely awakened in the night, shoved onto trains and sent somewhere into Siberia. Would our turn come soon?

Ernest, shortly after the German invasion of Poland, 1939

CHAPTER 4

Exile to Siberia

It was 3:00 a.m., a night in June, 1940. Ernest and I were awakened by a sharp knock at the thin door of the student apartment building where we were living. The building was formerly an orphanage operated by the Jewish community, which the Russians confiscated shortly after their occupation forces moved in. The rapping on the door came again, louder and more insistent.

"Who is it?" I called out, trying to collect my senses.

"Police. Open up!"

Still groggy from sleep, I opened the door to face a Russian policeman, accompanied by a plainclothesman.

"Yes? What do you want?" I asked apprehensively.

"Get your belongings together," the one in plain clothes ordered. "We are sending you both back home to your family."

Bewildered, but hopeful, we hastily did as we were told, and left with the intruders. We were unaware at the time, that "repatriation" was the commonly-used ploy to round up exiles for deportation to labor camps. Ernest and I were, of course, on the government's registration list. We were put aboard an open transport truck which was already full of people.

"Where do you suppose we're being taken?" Ernest asked

aloud to no one in particular.

"Probably to Hades!" a passenger crudely answered in his anger and frustration.

"They told us we were being sent back home," Ernest rebuked the man. "We are coming into the train station anyway."

"Everybody out! Move quickly! Jews keep together!"

The two of us tumbled out of the truck and tried to stay together as we were prodded along with the others by the guards. The railway station was jammed with thousands of Jewish refugees, some of whom I recognized, but was unable to reach. Armed guards prevented any milling around or attempts to leave the station, while other guards goaded people into railroad cattle cars. Thirty or forty terrified refugees were crowded into each car, which was furnished only with wooden bunks. There was no water and no toilet. My brother and I were shoved into a car along with many other frightened people, all fighting for space.

"Make your way to the wall," I shouted above the din, pushing Ernest ahead of me. "We'll be better off there than crushed in the middle of this mess."

Both of us were slim and strong, and managed to push our way to the side of the car. We fashioned a bed for ourselves, using our bundles of clothing for pillows. Still under the delusion that we were being transported back to our homeland, we settled down to endure the miserable conditions. The train embarked into the night and by morning was deep into Russian territory. Instead of traveling westward back to occupied Poland as was supposed, the hapless cargo of human beings was being taken eastward to Russia. Joyful homecoming expectations turned to horror when we realized that we had been victimized by another enemy. From that time on, our lives were a nightmare of uncertainty and ever-deepening despair.

The refugees spent an agonizing twenty-four days and nights on the train. Once a day, we were given some bread and a bucket of soup into which all dipped. We were not allowed to leave the railroad car to obtain extra food from the platform peddlers during the rare stops. Sometimes the Russians herded us through showers and disinfected our clothes at the major train stations. A hole in the floor of the boxcar, encircled by a blanket, sufficed for a toilet. From the terrible lack of sanitation, many people became ill and were removed from the train. What happened to them, no one knew.

The train finally stopped at Asino, near the Ob River. The exiles still alive numbered about three thousand.

"The train has stopped, Eliezer! Oh! They're opening the door! Do you think we're going to be shot?" Ernest, who was slightly taller than I, blinked at the daylight that suddenly flooded the car.

"At least we don't have to be first out." It was a thin try to calm my brother who had already had such an experience.

The passengers were ordered to get out, and for several days we camped in a nearby rolling meadow. The multitude was made up of whole Jewish families, single male Jews, and people who had associations with Jews in one way or another, marital, social, or business connections. Unlike the Germans who seemed to take sadistic pleasure in telling people where they were being sent, the Russians offered no clues. Speculation about our destination was the main topic of conversation among the exiles. My brother and I became friendly with a Jewish family from Lublin, a Mr. Landsman, his wife, and six children. Mr. Landsman was extremely apprehensive.

"I've heard we are going to Siberia to work in the coal or gold mines there," the former tradesman said morosely. "No one seems to know how families will be accommodated. My wife is not very strong, and we have so many little ones. I hope we will not be separated."

"Don't worry, Mr. Landsman," I encouraged. "The Russians will try to keep us contented workers. Surely they will keep families together for that reason."

"I hope you are right, young man. At least that is a positive thought."

While the exiles waited in the meadow camp, for what we did not know, the Russians fed us a coarse porridge containing spoiled meat that sickened many of the people. Determined to stay healthy, the Urbach brothers ate as little of it as possible. Meanwhile, more trains arrived and disgorged hundreds of new refugees. Eventually, a fleet of coal barges arrived, pulled by steamers on the Ob River. The wretched human cargo was loaded onto the barges, and for nine days, we lived and slept on bunks covered with black coal dust, or on top of the barge where the mosquitos ravaged those of us who preferred the mosquitos to suffocation below.

The barges docked at a clearing near a forest. We were all led to long barracks in the clearing. An officer announced, "You will live in this place. You will never leave this place. If you don't get used to it, you will not survive."

Youth and initial good health enabled Ernest and me to endure the ordeal of getting to the labor camp. The place was called Malinovka.

"So this is our 'home'!" I grimaced. "God help us!"

"I'm sure no one else will," Ernest added dolefully. "Do you think we will survive, Eliezer? It looks so hopeless."

"Yes, we are going to get out of here, Ernest. Be strong, and don't think bad thoughts. We'll just take it a day at a time."

I put my arm around my brother and shook him affectionately. Ernest was rigid with fear and despair, but my hopeful outlook was infectious, and seemed to gird up his morale.

The men who had the strength to labor were put to work rolling logs with their bare hands down to the river, where other people tied the logs into rafts which were floated downstream to a lumber mill. Those who did not work received only half a ration of food. Ernest and I were fortunate to be able to work, and even managed to exchange our extra clothes for bread and milk at a nearby village.

One day I had noticed some of the women from the camp bringing in bread, milk, and honey.

"Where did you get those foodstuffs?" I inquired.

"In Malinovka—the village down the road."

"But how did you buy it?" Since no one had legal tender, I wondered how the women did business with the villagers.

"We didn't buy it, we bartered for it," one of the women explained. "The village is very primitive. The people are mostly collective farm workers, and they have never seen the likes of our western 'luxuries.' They are most happy to trade food for articles of clothing—coats, shoes, underwear—whatever you want to give them."

"How is it you were allowed outside the camp to go to the village? I didn't know we could do that. Aren't the Russians afraid we will escape?" I asked naively.

"Escape? You must be joking! Don't try it, young man. You do not speak the language, you have no identification papers, and strangers are easily detected. You would stick out like a sore thumb and be caught immediately. The natives aren't foolish enough to try to help people like us on the loose, and a long prison term is guaranteed for such an attempt!"

"So much for that idea," I finished, after repeating the woman's advice to Ernest, "but let's go to the village to do some trading anyway."

❧

About six weeks after our arrival at the Malinovka camp, a hunger strike was initiated at another camp on the river. To keep the strike from spreading, the authorities removed the strikers, mixed them in with a number of exiles from Malinovka, and transported them all by barge to a place called Chermoshniki. This camp was located eight kilometers from Tomsk, the ancient capital of Siberia. My brother and I were among those sent to Chermoshniki.

Several hundred years ago, Siberia became a place of exile. Peter the Great sent the first political prisoners to Siberia in

1710. The vast, remote region, combined with long, extremely cold winters, makes escape virtually impossible. Leaving a prison compound for the wilderness meant almost certain death from the elements or wild beasts. It was a risk taken with little chance of success, but there were always a few who tried. The Czars and dictators of Russia made Siberia the graveyard of millions of exiles, enemies, and criminals. To be going there portended an ominous future for the barge passengers.

It was early September, 1940, and the uncompromising Siberian winter was approaching. Rain and snow pelted us as we entered Chermoshniki. A shabbily-built, one-room barracks furnished with fifty iron beds and straw mattresses was to be our dwelling place through the first Siberian winter. The only facilities were an outhouse, and a single clay stove for heat. No winter clothing was issued immediately, and only one blanket per person provided scanty protection from the cold drafts blowing through the cracks in the walls. Clothing soon stank and became infested with lice.

By now, approximately one million refugees were in exile, eighty to ninety percent of them Jewish. Awesome stories of Nazi treatment of the Jews filtered into the camp, tales of wholesale slaughter of men, women, and children. Evidence of Russian barbarity was not absent. Included among the ten thousand exiles at the Chermoshniki work camp were Russian peasants who had refused to join collective farms, former government employees, and other victims of Stalin's sweeping purges in the 1930's. Before the power struggle in Russia ended, nearly a million Communists were driven from the party, and millions of other Russians were imprisoned or executed. The children born to these people while in Siberia were set free.

The day after our arrival, all the newcomers were lined up.

"What do you think this is for?" Ernest whispered.

"They never tell you in advance, do they? The Russians like to keep us in suspense. Look, here comes the answer."

A Russian official, flanked by several assistants bearing what looked like medical equipment, entered the barracks.

"You will all be given anti-typhus injections," the official announced. "Please remove your shirts."

"Well, isn't that thoughtful of them already," I wisecracked. "At least we won't be dying of typhus here."

The injections were given in the shoulder, not a good place considering the next day's work detail.

The following morning, the work camp authorities separated the Jews from the Stalin era exiles, and ordered us to work out of doors, moving lumber in the icy weather. The "white nights" of the Siberian winter meant only one hour of darkness, and a fourteen-hour work day. Along with the other men, the two of us carried stacks of boards and railway ties on our shoulders, with only a little cotton pillow beneath the load, which hardly alleviated the pain. Our bodies were now thin and bony, and the skin became lacerated easily with the abrasion. Each worker was required to carry a certain number of boards a day to be paid, and the pay barely bought enough food to sustain us. The cafeteria at the work camp charged outrageous sums for soup, meat, and fish.

There were a few consolations at Chermoshniki. Germany and Russia were not yet at war, and correspondence was allowed. We wrote and received letters from home. Aunt Emma sent us packages of food. Mama often wrote her sons:

"Hold on and be strong! After the war, we will talk about our troubles together and be joyful."

A family from Cieszyn, by the name of Sussman, turned up in the camp. Mr. Sussman owned an ice-cream parlor in the town where I attended high school, and his son was one of my classmates. It was a happy reunion, and a morale boost to meet people from home.

"How did you get here?" I asked them.

"We were taken from Lvov about the same time I'd guess you two were picked up in Stanislav," was Mr. Sussman's melancholy reply. "We were brought directly here to Chermosh-niki without your side trip to Malinvoka. Some 'repatriation', nu?"

Also at Chermoshniki, I met a young German Jew named Kahane. His family were actually Polish Jews who had emigrated to Germany, but never changed their citizenship. In 1938, Hitler expelled Jews who were not German citizens, making refugees of them. Kahane lived with his elderly mother in the camp. When the mother became sick, she was taken to a hospital in Tomsk where she died. Kahane received a letter from the authorities informing him of his mother's death, and instructing him to come for the body. Permission for the burial had to be obtained from the proper bureau in Tomsk. Kahane asked me to accompany him on this difficult mission.

It was mid-winter, and an eight-mile walk to Tomsk. Unfortunately, we made the trip on Saturday, only to find the Burial Bureau closed on the weekend. On Monday, we went again. Space in the Jewish cemetery was granted, after which we looked for the Jewish community. People were needed to perform the traditional burial rites, and for prayers. An elderly Jew offered a pall with a Mogan David on it. I hired an old Russian to transport the body from the hospital on his horse-drawn sled. However, when we arrived at the hospital, we were told that the body had been removed to the morgue. Kahane became distraught.

"I can't go into the morgue! I am a Cohen!" he anguished.

"Never mind," I volunteered. "The Russian and I will get your mother. You wait here."

The Russian helped me carry a pine coffin which the Jewish community had provided, and the caretaker directed us to the body. It was a gruesome sight. Having laid in an unrefrigerated morgue for five days, the body was putrid and bloated. The old Russian threw a sheet over it, and we started to lift it into the coffin. Suddenly, the odor overwhelmed both of us, and I began to gag with nausea. We dropped the body on the floor.

"Let's go out for a breath of fresh air," the Russian

suggested.

"What is the matter?" Kahane was greatly agitated when we reappeared empty-handed. "Where is my mother?"

"It's all right. Just be patient. We'll have her in a few minutes," I reassured him, struggling for the courage to go into the morgue again.

The second attempt was successful. Two brave Jewish women performed the taharah (ceremonial washing and dressing of the body for burial), and the funeral procession went to the cemetery. Ten Jewish men had dug a shallow grave. The perma-frost was so thick and hard, it was almost impossible to penetrate it with picks and shovels.

The gray-haired elder who was in charge of the funeral began to intone the traditional prayer:

"O, merciful God, who dwells in eternity, may the soul of him or her be bound in a bond of life, and may he or she be a mediator for us and for all Israel. Amen."

I had heard this prayer many times before, without giving it much thought. In these bizarre circumstances, I questioned the words. How could this old lady be a mediator for anyone? "A bond for life?" She was more than dead. What life? The words of the prayer did not make any sense to me.

⚜

The winter season brought privation and sickness. During the year that Ernest and I lived at the work camp, nearly all of the older single men died of malnutrition and pneumonia. Those who did not keep clean or shave were the first to freeze and become sick. The younger men developed scurvy. Many of the exiles lost their will to live, and lapsed into a deep depressive state. Others took the hardships in stride, hoped for freedom, and battled for survival. I had always been healthy, and was endowed with a strong, stubborn will. I did not become seriously ill, but Ernest's physical condition deteriorated. We encouraged one another and clung to hope.

Relief came in September, 1941. The United States, Great

Britain, and Russia signed an agreement to free all Polish exiles, P.O.W.'s, and slave laborers in Russia. The refugees from the camp near Tomsk were taken by cargo train to Novosibirsk, then to Tashkent, capital of Uzbekistan.

The German-Russian alliance ended with Hitler's invasion of Russia in June, 1941. The Red Army could not stop Hitler's advance and German troops drove within a hundred miles of Moscow. Leningrad was under siege. Hundreds of thousands of freed exiles and Russians fleeing Hitler's armies were pouring into the "city of bread and sunshine." The climate of Tashkent was a marked contrast from the dismal cold of Siberia. The country was so arid that we joined the throngs sleeping in the open at the railway station square.

"Well, what do we do now, Eliezer?" my brother asked.

"I think somehow we have to leave Russia, but the question is, how? We have to put our heads to that, Ernest."

"You're right, I agree. There is no real freedom in a police state. We'll always be at the mercy of the Russians for something or other, and we haven't seen much mercy here. We have to get out."

As we sat propped against a wall discussing our plight, I scanned the crowd around us. Suddenly, I jumped to my feet.

"Of all things! Look over there, Ernest. Do you see a familiar Jewish face?

"Why, yes! It's Mr. Berger from Bielsko! What is he doing here?"

"Let's find out!"

We made our way through the throng toward Mr. Berger, and hailed him. Berger had been a wealthy lawyer in the neighboring town of Bielsko before the war. He was a member of an exclusive hunters club which used the forests and fields around Skoczow for their hunting expeditions. The club members often brought heaps of game killed in a hunt to Papa's restaurant and sold the prey to the peasants at the inn.

Mr. Berger was equally surprised to see the Urbach

brothers. His story was, by now, an all too familiar one. He had fled from the Germans, made his way to Russia, and was entrapped in the "repatriation" deception. He now had a scheme to get back to Poland, which he shared with us.

"A Polish army is being organized near Moscow to fight the Germans," Berger explained. "This may be our opportunity to escape. There are one hundred and fifty Polish Jews here ready to go. Do you want to join us?"

"Of course!" we answered without hesitation. "When do we leave?"

"On the first train to Moscow."

A ten-day train ride brought our Polish contingent of volunteers to Buzuluk in wintry November. We found lodging in an agricultural market which had no heat or sanitary conditions. We soon had lice in our hair and clothing again.

Ernest and I reported to the recruitment office with high hopes. We waited two weeks for a decision, sleeping in a covered bazaar. During that time, the recruitment office provided food for the prospective volunteers.

When our turn came to be interviewed, we learned to our great disappointment that the Polish army was not eager to enlist Jews.

"I am very sorry," the officer-in-charge informed us, "we can accept only Jews who served in the regular Polish army before the war. You will not be receiving any more food rations from us. Go your way. These papers entitle you to a train ride back to Tashkent."

The officer shoved the documents across his desk and dismissed us. The regulation eliminated many of the Jewish refugees who had come to enlist, leaving them destitute displaced persons.

Stunned, frustrated, and angry at our rejection, my brother and I walked slowly back to the train station.

"Damn the Polish Jew-haters!" I cursed. "They aren't fooling any of us with their stupid regulations. We've always been good citizens, but the Poles don't even want us to fight for them. They know this army is our ticket out of Russia, but they won't even grant us that!"

"Go your way!" Ernest mocked the official. "And what way would that be?"

"Where else? Back to Tashkent."

We returned to Tashkent with the continuing problem of survival. To earn money for food, we sought work harvesting cotton on a collective farm. Toiling from early morning to nightfall, neither Ernest nor I could reach the quota. We were undernourished and too weak to produce the required amount. Although the workers were issued grain to make flat barley cakes, many died of starvation and typhus.

After a week on the farm, I realized that we would starve to death there, too. We were gaunt with hunger and overrun with lice. At the ages of eighteen and twenty, we were already seasoned sufferers. We had spent more than a year of our lives defying death from cruel persecutors, either in flight or in labor camps. Nowhere in Russia could we expect to receive fair treatment. Filled with misery and desperation, weary and emaciated, we once again devised a plan of escape.

CHAPTER 5

Prison

While sitting in a dingy teahouse, Ernest's attention was captured by a wall-map.

"Eliezer! Look!"

"So, a map?"

"We are not far from Afghanistan!"

"Oh, I see! To be in Afghanistan would be better than to be here."

Carefully, we sketched a map of the area on a scrap of paper. Late that night, we made our way by train to the Amu Darya river on the Afghanistan border. As the train approached the river, we jumped from the moving cars, and rolled out of sight into the bushes. The area was heavily patrolled by Russian border guards.

After fifteen minutes of walking, we heard dogs barking in the distance.

"There must be a village ahead," I surmised.

"Let's hope those dogs are just friendly village mutts," Ernest added. "I think we'd better not get too close, just in case. How do we know we're going in the direction of the river?"

"By the stars. Look behind you. See the Big Dipper? We know by the map that we should be going south, so we keep the

Big Dipper behind us," I cleverly instructed my brother with the mock sagacity of an older brother.

"Now if we just had a boat, you could be a real navigator," Ernest came back at me, with his good-natured grin of old times.

I was grateful to see a glimmer of Ernest's cool sense of humor even briefly. He could always best me with his dry wit in the past. Beginning with his early traumatic experience when the war first began, Ernest's intelligent sense of reasonableness had been continually assaulted by the barbarity loosed upon innocent people, and the shock of it took its toll on his personality. His humor had been fine-tuned to our way of life before the war, and he found few ways to express it now. Neither could he function well with his life so much out of his own control. Always a sober-minded boy who took his responsibilities seriously, his activities were well ordered, and resiliency had never been required of him. Papa had rightly calculated our respective chances for survival, if circumstances had worked out in Ernest's favor.

We entered a cotton field about 4:00 a.m. Dawn was breaking, and the rising sun gave us another fix on our southerly direction. We had skirted the village, and now, emerging from the cotton field, we could see a Russian border garrison near the river. The guards on duty were dozing. For the next hour, we fought our way through a sea of tall reeds until we reached the water.

"We'd better take off our clothes for the swim, Ernest. Tie your clothes in a bundle and strap them to your back. Pack them as tight as you can. Maybe we can keep something dry if we don't get completely swamped."

It was October, and the water was very cold. We paddled valiantly until we reached what we assumed was the Afghanistan mainland.

Shivering with the cold, but exultant, Ernest shouted through his chattering teeth, "Hurrah for us! We're in Afghanistan! We're free!"

"Let's not celebrate yet," I cautioned. "Get dressed quickly. We have to move on to find shelter and dry out before we catch pneumonia."

Joy soon turned to dismay. We had not walked far until we discovered that our swim had landed us on an island lying in the confluence of two rivers, and we were still in Russian territory. We found the river we had intended to cross still before us.

"Oi vey! Look at that enormous river! You can't even see the other side! We couldn't possibly swim across that much water, Eliezer. We don't have the strength to do it." Ernest shivered at the thought.

"Well, we've got to try anyway. The Russians will get us here for sure. Come on, let's go swimming!"

The wind was whipping the water into rough waves, and the river current was swift. We made several desperate attempts, but never got more than a few yards from shore each time. It was hopeless.

For three days, we wandered around the area, eating grass and drinking river water to stay alive.

"We didn't plan this out well enough in advance," I commiserated. "From now on, no matter how desperate we are, we had better think things through before taking off. We have to know exactly what we are doing and where we are going. No more mistakes like this, nu?"

"That's true, Eliezer. I just hope there will be a next time. I'm so miserable and hungry, I can't think of any more plans right now."

As we sat cold and exhausted on the ground, suddenly the sound of barking dogs rent the air.

"The green hats are coming! They're coming after us!"

"Well, let them come. It will be a relief. At least we'll get warm and be fed." Ernest had a point.

Too weak to run or resist, we awaited our fate. A Russian patrol, led by a pack of snarling dogs, were soon upon us.

"You there! Do not move or we'll set the dogs on you!" one of the guards threatened. "Lie down on the ground!"

We were searched, tied up, and pushed into a patrol boat. At the border police station, our interrogation began.

"Who are you? Are you from Afghanistan?"

Terrorist activity in the country led the police to suspect that we were Afghans involved in this business.

"No sir," I spoke up. "We are Polish refugees, and have papers of release from Siberia."

"I see. May I examine your papers, please?"

The official carefully studied the soggy papers which we handed over to him.

"What are you doing here?"

"We were on our way to Stalinabad to look for work, and lost our way," I lied poorly.

"Stalinabad?" the police captain repeated. "Step over to this map on the wall and retrace your steps for us, please."

We were trapped. The train from which we had jumped did not go to Stalinabad, and the tracks were at least ten miles from the river. Neither was there a road anywhere near that we could have been traveling on. My story was an obvious fabrication.

"You are lying to us!" the official accused angrily. "Guard! Throw these two criminals into the dungeon!"

For three days, we were kept in a dank cellar beneath the building. Every few hours, night and day, we were brought up and interrogated again. Finally, ready to end this misery, we confessed to our "crime," and were sent to prison in Termez to await trial.

For six long months, Ernest and I languished in jail, and were kept in separate cells. We did not see each other again until the day of trial.

The courtroom itself was intimidating. The cold, gray room was sparsely furnished with pieces of dilapidated metal chairs and tables. No spectators were on hand to observe the administration of justice. In the center of the room against the far wall, the stern-faced judge sat behind his bench. Overhead hung two large pictures of Lenin and Stalin. A prison guard escorted the two of us to a standing place in front of the bench. The judge glared at us menacingly, and his heavy jowls began to move.

"You are charged with an illegal attempt to cross the border. Do you have anything to say for yourselves in this matter?"

"No, sir," we answered together, having decided hastily on the way to the courtroom that the less said the better. We would offer nothing in our defense.

"Two years imprisonment!" the judge growled in passing our sentence. "In the future, you will do well to remember that no one gets in or out of Russia without permission! Take them away."

Ernest broke down and cried on hearing the sentence. Two years sounded like an eternity to him. On the other hand, I was relieved that the term given was not more than two years. I thought we should count ourselves lucky to get off so lightly.

We were taken by train to a prison camp at Tashkent. The train cars were adapted for transporting prisoners and each car was packed with people. All compartments were equipped with locks and guarded. As I was entering a compartment, the Russian guard, shod in steel-capped boots, gave me a brutal kick in the back. My vertebrae sustained an injury that continued to cause discomfort for many years to come.

The prisoners were given no food or water during the long, slow trip to Tashkent. Conditions at the camp were deplorable. The inmates were a conglomeration of hard criminals, thieves, politicals, deposed Communists, embezzlers, Russian Jews, Estonians, Latvians, and rebel Caucasian tribesmen whose native dress set them apart. The tribesmen wore long coats, tall fur hats, and colorful woolen capes over their coats. Tashkent was a huge "transfer camp," a pool of slave labor. From here, trains were organized and filled with slave laborers who were taken to Siberia to work on various Russian projects, dams and canals, and in factories.

At the camp, bed bugs and lice scourged the flesh of the inmates. Every ten days, our heads were shaved, and our clothes deloused in steam kettles.

Ernest grew thinner and thinner. He was suffering from malnutrition and diarrhea, which caused such cramps in his bowels he could not eat.

"I'm not going to make it, Eliezer," he told me one afternoon. "I feel like I'm dying already. I'm never going to see Poland, or Mama and Papa, or Aunt Emma, or anybody else ever again."

"Of course you are going to make it through this, Ernest. We're going to be free soon. Just hold on. I'll try to find some help for you. You be thinking what you are going to do when we get back home while I look for a doctor. I won't be away long."

I located two Jewish doctors in the camp, Dr. Warshavsky, the head physician, and Dr. Litvinsky, a woman.

"My brother is very sick," I pleaded with the doctors. "He will die soon without treatment. Please send him outside right away. Is it possible?"

"Perhaps. Let's have a look at him," Dr. Warshavsky replied. "Take us to him and we'll see what can be done."

After examining Ernest, the two doctors intervened on his behalf, and sent him to a civilian hospital outside the camp. Although greatly relieved that Ernest was getting medical treatment, our separation filled me with anguish, and I could hardly bear his absence. I tried to induce sickness in myself by swallowing tobacco, hoping to be sent to the hospital so I could be with my brother. The attempt failed to get me hospitalized.

About one month later, a prison functionary appeared at my cell. Tenure in prison had earned the man administrative privileges.

"Are you Eliezer Urbach?" the old prisoner asked.

"Yes. What do you want?"

"I'm sorry to tell you this, but your brother has died in the hospital."

Shock and grief overwhelmed me. How could I live without Ernest? Together, the two of us had brought each other a measure of strength-giving hope and determination to live. Now I was alone. Scenes of our childhood flooded my mind. My brother and I were the happy, spoiled sons of our father's old age. Papa was proud and indulgent with us. Berta, our mother, had been delivered from spinsterhood by her marriage to Heiman Urbach, and her two sons represented God's blessing upon her. Her gratitude was reflected in devotion to her family. By the standards of the day, we were prosperous and comfortable. Ernest and I had grown up together in the secure love of our parents. I recalled one photograph, taken by Helena one sunny Sunday afternoon, that especially captured our faces as we were typically in person. On one side of Papa, I stood grinning like the perennial imp in the family, and on the other side, Ernest was caught with his countenance straight and serious. Ernest, I thought now, was certainly the most promising son, a good student, a violin player, religious, a consonant joy to our father. Why did Ernest die? The catastrophe sent my mind reeling, and I sobbed in utter devastation. My spirit was broken.

৵

Many prisoners died of typhus, scurvy, dysentery, and diarrhea. There were no effective medicines available—no antibiotics, no opiates to kill the pain, no fresh vegetables or fruits to prevent diet deficiency diseases. It was not uncommon for prisoners to lose all their teeth or to develop ulcers. Life was unbearable in the prison. Unless I got out soon, I knew there was no hope for my survival.

"What is the best way to get into the hospital?" I asked an inmate who had been in the prison long enough to know all the tricks.

"A fake fever and fainting usually does it."

"How can these be induced?"

"Boil some tobacco and drink it. That will knock you out. Good luck!" the man grinned knowingly, and hastened off down the hall to deliver bread rations.

I followed the inmate's instructions, but the concoction only nauseated me. As I stood in the infirmary line, I pretended to faint and fell to the floor.

"Pick this one up and get him out of here!" someone ordered.

Two other prisoners carried me to the infirmary. My poor condition gained me admission for ten days of rest and regular meals. However, the infirmary was so crowded, two men often shared one bed. One night, a sickly old man was dropped into my bed. The man was delirious from some unknown ailment, and kept crawling over me.

"Get off me, old man! What's the matter with you? Get off, I said!"

I pushed and shoved the writhing body again and again, unaware that the stranger was in the throes of death. In the morning, the man was dead.

Nevertheless, the brief respite from the prison cell strengthened me, and led to another improvement in my circumstances. My stay in the infirmary acquainted me with procedures there, and after my discharge, I applied for work as an orderly. I was accepted, and employed there for the next seven months. Two Jews, one a European named Kushner, the other a Bukharian called Gabrieloff, were medical corpsmen in the hospital clinic. They were both serving sentences for "speculation," buying and selling illegal merchandise.

"Pay attention, Urbach, and we'll teach you how to be a good orderly," Kushner offered. "The better job you do, the more chance you'll have to stay on the staff at Tashkent."

"What's the advantage of that?"

"Don't you know? Staff members are exempt from being shipped out with the labor forces. That's a big advantage, wouldn't you say?"

"Great! Show me all the techniques a good orderly should know. I learn very fast!"

Although my health improved somewhat while working in
the hospital, I knew that I was slowly dying of starvation and
disease. I had never taken Orthodox Judaism seriously, nor found
it meaningful to my life, and the prescribed prayers and
ceremonies gave homage to a God I did not know. But now, for
the first time, I consciously prayed:

"God of my father and my mother, forgive me if it was my
fault that Ernest died. Maybe I did wrong to try to cross that
border. If we hadn't tried to do that, maybe Ernest would not
have died in prison. I feel responsible, but I don't know what to
do about it now. If I am to die also, please, God, let me die a free
man, and not in this filthy prison. There will be no one here even
to close my eyes. Oh, God, I don't know what to do."

Just a few months before my prison term at Tashkent would
have been completed, I made a desperate and ill-advised move.
Certain that I would die of starvation long before the time came
for my release, I succumbed to a scheme to get more bread. A
fellow Polish prisoner approached me one day.

"Friend, how would you like to join me in a little
enterprise?"

"What are you talking about?"

"I've figured out a way to make counterfeit food coupons.
We sell them and buy extra bread. Are you interested?"

"Why not? We're going to die here anyway, one way or
another."

The coupons were precious items in the prison, and their
acquisition was often a matter of life and death. The methods to
achieve it varied, but staying alive was the paramount concern of
all the inmates.

Despite all the trouble I had seen, I was still only twenty
years old, and too inexperienced to engage in such dangerous
traffic. Predictably, I was soon caught in the illicit coupon
business, beaten, and sent to the "calaboose," close quarters
under strict arrest.

The calaboose was a poorly-lit room six feet wide and

twenty feet long in which as many as twenty people were incarcerated. Under such conditions, human beings were reduced to bestiality. There were no chairs, beds, or mattresses. The men slept on the bare floor. The toilet was a barrel in one corner of the room. The stench was nauseating.

When I was shoved into the calaboose by the guard, several gaunt, wall-eyed prisoners approached me.

"You there, do you have any tobacco?" a toothless, foul-smelling inmate asked, as he circled the new prey.

I shuddered at the whole scene I had just entered. The exposure to such coarseness and cruelty was still sending shock waves through my young mind.

"No, I don't have any tobacco. I've just been transferred from the prison at Tashkent. I brought nothing with me."

The prisoners hissed in disbelief, and began to slap me around.

"Come on now, you pipsqueak! What do you have to share with us?" the apparent leader demanded with mock civility. "Search him!" he ordered the others, making sure he got to my pockets first.

I was crudely searched, and, finding nothing of value in my possession, the inmates pushed me into a corner so hard, I crumpled against the wall by the toilet barrel.

"All newcomers get to sleep by the barrel," one of the men proclaimed. "Hope you like the smell! That's the way we initiate people into our exclusive club!" Sadistic laughter followed the assignment of my sleeping quarters.

This was my introduction to the "shpahnah." With the exception of a few Jews, most of the prisoners in the calaboose were native Russians. Selling food on the black market warranted up to five years in prison. The penalty for petty thievery was one year; for stealing government property, five to six years. Hundreds of thousands of young Russian men spent their lives in and out of prison. They lived on the streets and robbed for a livelihood. Some stole because they had no choice; others, because they were lazy or too demoralized to pursue legitimate means. In prison, these professional thieves were known as the "shpahnah." They were cruel, unscrupulous men, for whom human life had no value.

On a bench by the wall, the calaboose thieves and bullies sat playing cards. They made the cards by cutting up newspaper to the proper size, and pasting the pieces of newspaper together with a glue-like starch which they concocted from chewing black rye bread. To draw spades and clubs on the cards, they burned the rubber on their slipper soles, made of old rubber tires, and mixed the burnt material with spittle. To make a red dye for hearts, they feigned sickness and coaxed an orderly to give them a red pill from the outpatient clinic. A yellow pill was used to draw diamonds.

For hours, these man played Twenty-One, gambling for a piece of bread or sugar, or for a new prisoner's belongings. If a new man refused to hand over his suit or other desirable possessions, he was beaten by the "shpahnah." Consequently, the thieves were reasonably well dressed, although sometimes they lost their clothes to each other in a card game.

The "shpahnah" would stop at nothing to obtain extra food coupons. The coupons were distributed by guards or prison functionaries, and were required to receive a mug of soup and bread brought each day. The prisoners sat routinely against the wall in rows of four. The first man in each line was handed the coupons for all the men in his row. He was supposed to tear off his own and pass the rest down the line. Often, the leader stole all of the bread coupons for himself. The men who then received only the remaining soup coupons were doomed to starve, since there was little nourishment in the watery soup. Another method the "shpahnah" used to get more food coupons was to prop up the body of a dead prisoner in their row to collect the deceased person's allotment. Dead bodies were kept under bunks for several days for such purposes. Although the calaboose was disinfected and the barracks showered down every ten days, disease and malnutrition took a heavy toll of lives.

Having lost the privilege of being on the staff at the Tashkent camp by my transgression there, and being too weak to work, I was sent to a camp for invalids after the confinement in the calaboose. The horrors of the new camp, called Yalangach, far exceeded any I had experienced yet. It was a place of sub-human existence, where the weak and infirm were expected to die anyway. After several months at Yalangach, I became a watchman in a men's dormitory. I swept floors, fetched water, and was also responsible for the personal belongings of inmates. Rampant stealing made the latter duty a hopeless and brutal task.

"You miserable dog!" the frequent tirade went. "You let my bread (or whatever it was) get away! I'll take your head off for that! You are a no-good watchman!"

Venting their rage, fellow prisoners often beat me for their losses. I was also suffering from colitis and malnutrition, and could not keep food in my stomach. I was losing my will to live.

One day, a woman doctor whom I had met in the Tashkent hospital, came to Yalangach. She recognized me on the street in the camp, and came over to talk. Her name was Dr. Nazarova.

"You look quite sickly," the doctor observed immediately. "Quite sickly, indeed, far too thin. How ill are you?"

"I'm in very bad shape, Dr. Nazarova, and if I have to stay here much longer, I don't think I'll live."

"How long have you been here?"

"About four months, I think. I've lost track of time."

"Come to my office this afternoon. I will get you out of here."

The doctor left me standing in dumb amazement. My prayer had been answered!

The meeting with Dr. Nazarova was providential. The woman owed me a great favor from our days at Tashkent when I was an orderly. The clinic where she worked was short of medical help.

"We need more doctors here very badly," Dr. Nazarova complained bitterly at a staff meeting. "Most of them are serving the army, and there are none available for the camps. It's a terrible situation."

"I know where there is a good doctor and he is available," I volunteered.

"You do? Where?"

"In the common prison ward. He is Polish, and a qualified physician. He could be a great help to you."

"That's an excellent idea! I'll have him transferred to the clinic at once! Thank you very much for the information."

Dr. Nazarova got more than she expected. A romance developed between the Polish doctor and Nazarova. A large, blond, warm-hearted woman, she was now going to repay me for the happy outcome at Tashkent.

"I'm sending you to work in the prison pharmacy," Dr. Nazarova announced when I reported to her office. "The better food there will strengthen you. Let me know how you do. I hope the change will help you get well soon."

"Thank you very much, Dr. Nazarova. I appreciate what you have done for me. I'll try to do a good job."

The pharmacist for whom I was to work was a woman about thirty years old. Unfortunately, my predecessor had been a young, strong Russian with whom the pharmacist had an intimate relationship. The Germans were attacking Stalingrad, and Russians were being taken from the prisons to serve in the army. Being able-bodied, the pharmacist's lover was sent to the front.

"Who are you?" the pharmacist asked when I appeared at the laboratory.

"I'm your new helper. Dr. Nazarova sent me."

"Don't be joking!" the woman smirked. "You're dying! You'll be of no good use to me. Get lost, you scrawny creature. Go back to the prison and finish dying!"

The jeers fell like whip lashes on my skeletal frame. I sagged under the verbal abuse momentarily, but rallied to make what I thought was probably an empty threat.

"We'll see about that! I'll be back here soon whether you like it or not!"

By the time I got back to Dr. Nazarova's office, I was weeping in humiliation and despair.

"She wouldn't let me in, Dr. Nazarova. She told me to go back to prison and die. Am I condemned to die at age twenty?"

"You go right back to the pharmacy and tell the woman that I will call her," Dr. Nazarova directed.

The telephone rang shortly after I returned to the pharmacy and delivered the message. The pharmacist's face reddened as she listened to Dr. Nazarova. When she hung up the telephone, she turned to me and said tersely, "All right, you're on. Go wash bottles."

For two months in the pharmacy, I washed bottles, boiled herbs, and weighed and wrapped medicinal powders. A Jewish woman prison functionary who worked in the laboratory, sometimes shared part of her meals to augment my rations. My health gradually improved with the better living conditions, so that by the time I was to be considered for a medical discharge, I was nearly disqualified.

Every morning the prisoners were lined up for inspection. Prison officials came with a list of those who were to be released that day. As their names were read, the men selected for release moved to another line. Only the ones who were very sick, crazy, or dying were on the list. The cost of burial was thus avoided by the prison administration. As I stood in the second line, a reviewing doctor stopped and looked me over.

"What is he doing here?" the doctor asked his attendant. "He looks pretty healthy to me. His name must have been put on the list by mistake."

Dr. Nazarova stepped up quickly to my defense.

"No, sir, it is not a mistake. This young man is my patient.

He has suffered from malnutrition too long. His condition is irreversible. He will surely not live long."

"Very well, Dr. Nazarova. We accept your medical opinion even though the boy looks as if he might be recovering."

In Summer, 1943, after twenty months in prison, I was set free.

CHAPTER 6

Free?

I was released from prison wearing cloth slippers, prison trousers, and an undershirt. Having no hair from the regular prison shaving, I carried an old piece of towel to cover my head to protect it from the hot summer sun. The prison authorities gave me thirty rubles, a piece of bread and some dried salted fish. I was unable to eat the food because of continuous diarrhea. And I had nowhere to go. Freedom had something in common with imprisonment—survival.

I joined several other freed prisoners who broke into some unattended storage bins enclosed by a barbed iron fence just outside the main prison walls. We stole some salted fish, hoping to barter the fish for more edible food or money. At a nearby market, I exchanged the fish for bread and sour milk. The milk quieted my inflamed bowels, but the bread only aggravated my starved condition.

At a railway station in Tashkent, I made friends with a Polish P.O.W., just released from a prison camp in the north.

"Where are you headed?" the new acquaintance wanted to know.

"Bukhara."

"Bukhara? How come? Do you know someone there?"

"No, but I met a Bukharian Jew in prison who told me that many Jews live in Bukhara and have very little trouble with the Moslems. This fellow said that the Jews are pretty much left free there. Sounds like a good place for me to go for that reason alone, wouldn't you say so? Besides, I have no other place to go. You're welcome to join me if you care to do so."

"Why not? Might as well have company going somewhere. I'm not Jewish, but I've been displaced by the war, too. I'll be happy to come along with you."

Without tickets, we boarded a train traveling to Bukhara, about 300 miles east. However, the trip was aborted when the conductor discovered we were unpaid riders, and made sure that we were ousted from the train the next morning.

"I guess Bukhara was too ambitious a goal," I concluded. "Now what do we do?"

"I suggest we do a sensible thing and go to the nearest police station. We can neither apply for work nor travel around the country freely without proper papers. To get those, we have to show our prison release papers to the police. Maybe they can tell us where to look for work as well."

"You're right, my friend. As free men, we should do sensible things!" I thought that was rather a humorous remark considering our circumstances.

At the police station, we obtained the necessary documents, and were directed to a collective farm for employment and lodging.

After several hours of walking, we arrived at the farm, exhausted and hungry. The overseer sent us to a field of tomatoes where we spent the rest of the day working. When we returned to the farm, expecting to be fed for our labor, the overseer had only a sharp reply to our request for food.

"Go eat tomatoes!"

"Oi! I can't eat tomatoes! The acid will eat up my stomach! Don't you have something else?" I implored.

"Sorry, Polack, it's tomatoes or nothing."

It had to be nothing. Not wanting to exacerbate the painful condition of my digestive tract, I went without food.

The lodging was also a disappointment. That chilly night, there was no place to sleep but on the open veranda of the farm office. Still clad only in a prison undershirt, and racked with hunger, I shivered through the night. At dawn, a woman came to wash the windows facing the veranda. I stood up and saw my reflection in the shining glass. I hardly recognized myself. The face of a skeleton was staring back at me. I was so emaciated, every bone protruded from the skin.

"I look like a corpse," I thought to myself. "I'll soon have to be buried."

While my Polish friend slept, I pondered my chances for survival on the farm. If I stayed, I could expect to die of starvation. Furthermore, I had learned that the farm was owned by transplanted Ukrainians who were notorious Jew-haters.

"God," I again implored the nebulous power whose help I was beginning to trust, "I'm going to die on this farm. What should I do?"

In my heart, I felt sure I received an answer. I was to leave this place.

It was an hour's walk in the morning mist to the railway station. I boarded the first train going east, without a ticket as usual. The train was already rolling when the conductor entered and began to ask the passengers for their tickets. Before my turn came, I bolted the car, and was pursued by the conductor up and down ladders and over the roofs from carriage to carriage, a veritable Keystone cops chase.

Unexpectedly, the train stopped at a bridge. Armed guards boarded the train.

"All passengers without tickets will detrain at once! Out! Out!" The guards brandished their guns and quickly rounded up the irregular passengers.

The train had been intercepted twenty miles from the nearest town. I found myself stranded in the hot noonday sun along with fifteen other people. I followed lamely as the group started walking to the next railway station. I was weak from not having eaten the night before, and painful hunger spasms tore through my innards. I picked up some discarded fruit peelings from the ground and ate them, and from a roadside cornfield, I stripped off ears of corn and devoured them. I was far behind the group now and walking alone.

Two elderly men ambled along the road just ahead. I caught up with them and introduced myself. The men were residents of the state of Uzbekistan, one of the states of the Soviet Socialist Republic, located in central Asia. Both Uzbeks had recently been freed from prison. They spoke broken Russian, a language I had learned to speak in prison.

"I just got out of a working battalion," one of the men commented, tight-lipped about naming his offense, which probably meant that it was political, and he had learned to keep his mouth shut.

The other man was a Moslem mullah, and more talkative.

"I've been five years in prison for refusing a government order that conflicted with my religion. In Russia, one must choose between following Allah or Lenin."

I had never met a Moslem before, and was interested in what the mullah had to say about religious persecution in Russia.

"You can't practice your religion in Russia?"

"Neither Moslem, Christian, nor Jew can practice religion in Russia. Lenin is god, and Communism is the state religion. We are all persecuted for our different faiths. Jews are double cursed, once because they are Jews, and again because they won't all give up their faith in God. Are you a religious Jew?"

I hesitated to answer the mullah's question. At this point, I neither wanted to affirm my Jewishness, nor reveal that despite my inability to practice the only religion I knew, I had a feeling I had been praying to the God of my fathers. The safest thing was a negative reply.

"I'm not interested in religion itself, but I'm sorry to hear that there is no freedom of religion in Russia. That's a sad situation. People ought to be able to worship as they please."

"That's quite true, young man," the mullah allowed, "but bear in mind that the Communists intend to stamp out all religion. They are building a godless state here, and they will do away with anybody who persists in believing 'religious nonsense,' as they call it."

About 5:00 p.m., we reached a small town. Awaiting the train, we passed the time in a teahouse. I joined my companions in sitting on the floor, an Uzbek tradition, and they ordered tea. In their bundles, the Uzbeks were carrying flatcakes of native bread, called "nan," which they shared with me. As we sat drinking tea, two more customers entered the teahouse.

"Ah, ya!" the mullah whispered. "Look at the important people!"

"Communist party officials, no doubt," the other Uzbek clued me in. "Who else dresses like that, and gets that kind of treatment?"

The two Russians standing at the entrance were well dressed in civilian suits, and looked around the room with an officious air. One of them snapped his fingers toward the lady proprietor. She seemed to know exactly what the signal conveyed, and promptly brought out a table and chairs. Just as quickly, she served them a pot of tea. Laughing and talking boisterously, the Russians opened a parcel which they had brought with them. It contained loaves of expensive European bread, a sight the three of us on-lookers had not seen for ages.

"Look at that bread!" I wheezed. "From the black market for sure." My companions nodded in agreement.

As the Russians passed the parcel around the table, a piece of the bread fell to the floor. Incredibly, neither of the men made an effort to retrieve it. Eyeing the bread hungrily, I crossed the room and picked it up. Stepping back quickly out of range of the Russian boots, I waited for the reaction. Surprisingly, the

Russians did not seem to mind. Instead, they struck up a conversation with me.

"What is a young man like you doing with those old Uzbeks?"

"I was just released from prison, and these are my only friends."

"What were you in prison for?"

"Stealing bread," I quipped with a grin, and hoped the Russians had a sense of humor.

The Russians were in a good mood and laughed at my brash joke. Apparently, the sight of a half-starved youth also elicited some compassion. To my surprise, one of them handed me a ten ruble bill.

"Here, you young tramp, go buy yourself some bread."

"Thank you sir. You are very kind."

Not wanting to push my luck, I backed away and returned to my two companions, and proudly deposited the chunk of bread on the floor between them.

"Compliments of the Russians! Take some, please."

I was happy to have something to share with them in appreciation for their friendliness to me. The good bread provided a few moments of simple pleasure, and turned the conversation to pre-war days when such a tasty treat was available to common people.

At 2:00 a.m., a train rumbled into the station. The three of us scrambled aboard, and promptly lost one another in the crowd. The train was full of women toting produce to market, families enroute to visit relatives, and other miscellaneous travelers. The passengers were pressed together even between the cars and on the train steps.

Again, I was chased by the conductor because I had no ticket, but this time, I found a hiding place and avoided being caught. I wrapped myself around the ventilator chimney on top of the train. When the train stopped, I left my hiding place just long enough to steal food and water from the platform vendors, and then jumped back onto the train as it pulled out of the station.

Hunger gnawed at me constantly. I was a pitiful sight, bedraggled, emaciated, and my hair was still stubble from the prison shaving. The top of my head was badly sunburned from riding on the roof of the train. I was reduced to begging for bread or money, and occasionally, sympathetic people were moved to give something to me. I was going nowhere in particular, and barely existing. Having to beg brought me to the lowest point in my life.

Riding trains was too hazardous. A typhus epidemic had taken the lives of many passengers that year. The disease spread rapidly in the crowded conditions, and I did not want to fall a nameless victim of lice. I knew that I could not survive much longer alone. A Jewish community was my best hope for substantial help to get my life together.

When the train stopped at the station just outside of Gortshakova, while looking for food on the platform, I was startled to hear a large group of people speaking Polish. Many of them were Jewish, and I approached them eagerly.

"Excuse me," I interrupted in my native language. "Could you tell me what you are all doing here?"

"We are all enlistees in a Polish corps being mobilized by the Russians to fight on the German-Russian front," one explained. "Eventually, we hope to get back to Poland this way. The Russians are routing the Germans now, and the front is moving westward. Do you want to join us?"

"No, thanks," I declined. "I don't think that's for me. But good luck to you. I hope you make it home."

The offer to join this Polish army did not interest me in the least. Ernest and I had tried that route once before, and I still resented our rejection. Furthermore, I was in no physical condition to be a soldier, and had no desire to become Communist cannon fodder. Before leaving the group, I asked one more question.

"Are there any Jews living in the vicinity of Gortshakova?"

"If you are looking for Jews, you should go to the hospital. Some of the doctors there are Jewish."

Hoping this was a good lead, I found the hospital. The first person I encountered was a Polish Jew, a dentist who was working in the hospital as a medical doctor.

"Sir," I began abruptly, "my name is Eliezer Urbach. I am a Polish Jew, and have just been released from prison. I am ill, and have no place to go. Can you tell me where the local Jews live?"

"You do look as if you could use some help," the dentist responded, eyeing the wretched figure before him. He scribbled an address on a small piece of paper.

"This is my home. Go there now, and we'll see what we can do for you. I'll call my wife and tell her you are coming."

When I arrived at the home address, the dentist's common-law wife, a nurse, took me in and gave me a peach and a piece of bread.

"Do you know any Bukharian Jews? I inquired, after we had talked awhile. "I have met some elsewhere and they were very kind to me."

"Yes, as a matter of fact, there is a community of Bukharian Jews in Gortshakova, not too far from here. They have a reputation for generosity. I'm certain some of them will help you."

"Thank you very much for your hospitality and assistance. Please convey my thanks also to your husband. I'll be leaving now to find the Jewish community you have mentioned. The sooner I get help, the better, you understand? Thank you again."

"It was no trouble at all. Goodbye. I hope you find what you are looking for."

The nurse's parting words stuck in my mind as I made the short trip to Gortshakova. What was I looking for? I really did not know . . . perhaps just a city where I could find peace.

❧

Gortshakova was a small town named for the Russian Czar's general who conquered the caliphate of Bukhara in the 1800's. The large land mass which lies between the Caspian Sea and the Tien Shan Mountains was formerly known as Turkestan. In its early history, much of it belonged to the Chinese Empire. The followers of Genghis Khan swept through the area in the 1200's. During the next two centuries, Bukhara and Samarkand became centers of Moslem culture. Russia began to extend its rule to western Turkestan in the 1600's, and by the 19th century, most of the territory was under Russian authority. The little town of Gortshakova reflected all of this history in an old world, Oriental way of life. Although most of the people were Moslems, the Jews were unmolested and free to pursue their chosen vocations.

Arriving there in late afternoon, I chose a house at random in the Jewish neighborhood, and knocked at the door. The head of the household, a Bukharian Jew, answered the door, and waited for me to identify myself.

"Good afternoon, sir. I am a Jewish refugee, from Poland originally. I have spent many months in Siberian prison camps, and am now destitute. I need food, lodging, and work. Can you help me? My name is Eliezer Urbach."

The Bukharian sized up the strangely-clad starvling on his doorstep. Evidently, he concluded that I was too weak to be dangerous, and too candid to be suspicious.

"Come in, and we'll talk about it," he invited.

The Bukharian householder listened with great compassion as I explained my circumstances in more detail.

"The Jews here are all struggling to make a living," he explained when I had finished my story. "It's impossible to support a family on the income from one job. I myself work as a department store salesman during the day, and a dental technician in the evenings. I have a wife and one daughter only. Larger families find it very difficult to keep body and soul together. On the other hand, we have not suffered the indignities that you have. The minyan meets here tomorrow. Few synagogues are

allowed to function, so we gather in our homes. I'm sure the
congregation will find the means to help you. Please stay with us
for a while and rest. Now, please meet my wife and daughter. I'll
call them from upstairs."

Miriam, the daughter, was about my age, and quite attractive. Her features were a combination of Oriental and Jewish
heritage. High cheek bones and lovely eyes were framed by a
cascade of long black hair, making her seem more diminutive
than she actually was. Despite my jolting appearance, she met
me graciously, and accepted my apology for looking so unpresen-
table. She reminded me of the well-bred Jewish girls in Skoczow,
who were groomed by their mothers to be desirable wives. Under
other circumstances, I might have been more interested in her,
but at the moment, I was swaying on wobbly legs, half alive, and
thinking only of food.

Sonja, the girl's mother, was equally cordial and considerate.
With motherly warmth, she took the rescue initiative.

"Come into the kitchen, Eliezer. I have just cooked a pot of
rice. You are welcome to eat some of it, and from the looks of you,
you could use something that will stick to your ribs. After you
have eaten, I'll show you a little bed in our anteroom where you
can sleep. The accommodations aren't royal, but at least it's quiet
there."

I was overwhelmed with the family's kindness. That night, I
thanked God for leading me to these good people. For the first
time in many months, I felt a measure of peace, and remembered
my father's blessing, bestowed nearly four years ago.

⚜

The next morning, an international minyan of refugees and
local Jews gathered for prayer in the Bukharian's home. After
reciting the morning and mourner's prayers, the participants
took up a collection for me. There were two hundred rubles in the
hat. I was extremely grateful their sacrificial generosity, and
never forgot it.

I stayed two weeks with the Bukharian Jews, then returned

to the small hospital in Gortshakova to seek a job. The Jewish woman doctor who headed the staff suggested that I look for work at a factory which prepared dried fruits and vegetables for the Russian army. On arriving at the factory, the administrator who interviewed me was brief.

"You are obviously too sick to work here. My advice to you is to go back to the hospital and check in as a patient. When you have gained some weight, come back and I'll see if we can use you."

Actually, I was relieved at this dismissal, because I knew that I did not have the strength to do hard work, and I was not eager to take abuse for poor performance. Once again, I felt a providential hand was on my life. On the way back to the hospital, I realized in an enlightened moment that thanking God for unexpected blessings had become a habit. Perhaps I was not as irreligious as I had imagined myself during adolescence.

At the hospital, I reported the advice given by the factory administrator.

"The man was right," the head doctor agreed. "Forgive me, I should have made the same diagnosis. We will admit you to the hospital for treatment and rest until your health improves."

The doctor called in the small staff and gave them orders.

"Give this man a double portion of bread and all the food we can spare for the next month, and watch over his recuperation."

After several years of extreme deprivation and hardship, I had a clean bed, wholesome food, and friends. A nurse's aide, a 40-year-old Estonian woman, showed great compassion for me, saying that I resembled her own son, whose whereabouts she did not know. She mothered me, and brought fresh produce from a farm every day to add to my diet. My health improved rapidly, and soon the hospital employed me as a night watchman.

Some weeks later, the hospital director summoned me to his office.

"Yes, sir, what can I do for you?"

"The County Health Department has ordered me to recruit students for a course in disinfection at Tashkent. You seem to have a natural bent for medical work, and I must say, the trade might prove valuable to you. Would you like to take the course?"

"Let me think it over, sir, and I'll let you know tomorrow, if that's all right with you."

"Of course, but think over this opportunity carefully. At the institute you will be taught the rudiments of chemistry, and both personal and industrial hygiene procedures. You will learn how to disinfect and de-insect clothes, rooms, latrines, and stores. Because of the war, these skills are in great demand in both the military and civilian sectors. Employment will be assured."

"Thank you for thinking of me as a candidate for the institute. I'll be back to see you early in the morning with my decision."

The decision was not too difficult to make. I only needed time to adjust to the thought of moving on. I enjoyed my new friends and the pleasant environment, but still felt like a stranger in a strange land, rootless and restless. The course at the institute did sound interesting and could lead to a higher level of employment. I consented to go, and soon thereafter, set out for Tashkent with one monstrous loaf of bread, and official papers admitting me to the medical institute.

Study always came easy when I applied myself, and learning the formulas and procedures stimulated the mind that had been in survival limbo for so long. Another bonus was the acquisition of a new friend, the only other Jewish boy at the institute, a lanky, light-hearted fellow with blondish curly hair, blue eyes, and an infectious grin.

"What's your name?" he asked the first day of my arrival.

"Eliezer. What yours?"

"Jewish relatives, eh? Like mine—I'm Aaron. Glad to meet you. Where are you from?"

"Poland. Hitler invited me to leave."

"Likewise. I used to be from Romania. Now my home is in Samarkand. I was working in a health institution there and my superior came up with the disinfection course idea. I was bored with my job and accepted the invitation. How about you?"

"Well, I wasn't exactly bored, but thought I'd like a change anyway. And I needed to learn a trade. If you'd like, we can study together."

"Great idea! I could use some help . . . never was much good at studies. See you in class!" Aaron waved off, and whistled a merry ditty all the way across the grounds to the dormitory.

During the six months at the institute, we were often underfed. Room, board, and tuition were free, but the food supply was short. However, Aaron had a talent for stealing food from the bazaars, so we were not completely famished. By graduation, we had become inseparable friends. Aaron was special, a kindred spirit, and the most compatible friend I had known since high school days. He filled a great void in my life at the time, and his buoyant companionship helped hold my deep loneliness at bay.

After completing the course in disinfection, Aaron and I discussed employment possibilities.

"Let's go to Samarkand now, Eliezer."

"Why to Samarkand? What's the big attraction there?"

"Well, in the first place, I want to go home. In the second place, there are many Jews in Samarkand, and you'll like my friends. And the third reason is that I'm sure we can find a good job there. You'll see. Besides, what is there for you in Gortshakova, that dinky little town?"

"Whatever you say, Aaronchik," I laughed at his sales pitch. "I've already said goodbye to Gortshakova. When do we leave for your Samarkand?"

I did not believe I had an alternative. Aaron was my only friend, and instinct prevailed over design. Neither were there any circumstances in my life at the time that offered anything better than Aaron's plan.

We left for Samarkand by train, and went directly upon arrival to the Department of Health to present our certification papers for employment. We were accepted immediately, but our assignment was a shock. Expecting to work in the city, where we would find interesting friends and entertainment, we were chagrined to learn that we were to be stationed fifty miles from the city in the remote Tien Shan Mountains.

A horse-drawn cart carried us to the isolated disinfection station. The director, a Jewish man named Kozloff, greeted his two new workers.

"I'm glad to see that the Department of Health has not forgotten us. We have been asking for help for some time. You are a most welcome sight. Let me show you to your quarters, and then I'll instruct you in the use of the disinfecting equipment we have here."

Kozloff took us directly to a rustic, one- room hut. A small, woodburning stove provided heat. There was no electricity, and no water. Two mattresses on the floor were to be our beds. The hut was already inhabited by a gnarled old Uzbek whose job was to guard the supplies. Greatly disappointed with the accommodations, we soberly followed Kozloff back to the station, where the director immediately began to demonstrate the tools of the trade: a small container attached to a hose to spray disinfectant, a manual steel pulverizer, a hand pump, lysol, carbol, and soap.

"Are you ready for your first assignment?" Kozloff asked us the next morning.

"I think we can handle the equipment all right," I told him. "What is the job?"

"We have a request to disinfect the horse stable on a collective farm. It's not far from here. I've sketched a map for you. Load up then, and get along." Kozloff gave us each an encouraging pat on the shoulder, and disappeared into his office.

The stable was not a pleasant beginning, and the second assignment was even more depressing. We were sent to de-insect a military hospital for invalids, mostly amputees. The patients cursed us as we shook a foul-smelling power into the lice-infested beds. The sight of those young soldiers with missing feet, legs, and arms haunted my mind long afterward.

In payment for our work, we were given a small wage, and one full meal per day, consisting of porridge or soup with a little meat in it, and bread. We were constantly hungry, and once broke into the old Uzbek's winter cache of dried mulberries.

"This seems like a rotten thing to do, Aaron. The old man is hungry, too, don't you know?" I objected half-heartedly.

"Do you want to starve to death up here?" Aaron retorted. "Shut up and fill your pockets. We'll bring the old man something special the next time we go in for supplies."

Life at the disinfection station was bleak and lonely. We virtually had no contact with the outside world most of the time. It was hardly a satisfactory existence for two young cosmopolites. The situation suddenly changed when Aaron received a letter one day.

"Ho! Guess what, Eliezer. I've been drafted into the Russian army! The letter says I'm to report for duty right away. Well, at least I'll get out of this God-forsaken place. I really do hate to leave you here, but what can I do? Can I refuse to go? They would shoot me for that. I have to leave tomorrow for Samarkand."

"I understand, Aaronchik. You don't have a choice. You know I'll miss you, but take care of yourself, and maybe we can get together again after the war. I'll hold on at the outpost for a while, until I decide what to do next. I don't think I can stay long here without your company."

Working alone after Aaron's sudden departure, I was miserable and dejected. I made a trip to Samarkand the next day to replenish the supplies for the outpost. On the way back, I met Aaron and some other jaunty draftees walking down the road from the mountains on their way to the induction center.

"Hey! Eliezer!" Aaron called out. "Why don't you come with us?"

"Me? In the Russian army? No, thanks!" I shouted back.

In view of the treatment I had received at the hands (not to mention boots) of Russian soldiers, the idea seemed preposterous. I trudged disconsolately past the entourage of young men with my load of provisions. Suddenly, my knees went wobbly. Having been stripped of home, family, and country, the thought of being completely alone in the world again was unbearable. I delivered the supplies to the station outpost, packed my few possessions, and headed for the recruitment office to enlist.

CHAPTER 7

Under the Red Flag

After months of hand-to-hand combat in the streets of Stalingrad, the Russians had finally surrounded the German army in the city in February, 1943. Stalingrad was the turning point in the war for the Soviet Union. The Germans lost almost an entire army in the battle, and were greatly weakened by their losses and inadequate supplies.

At the time I enlisted, the Red army had begun to push the Germans from Soviet territory, and were pursuing them relentlessly. I went before the military commission at Samarkand to volunteer my services. I was given a brief physical examination. Doctors lifted my shirt to check for boils and skin diseases.

"Are you in good health?" one of the doctors inquired.

"Yes, sir." I think I must have smiled wryly at the question, as my long struggle to stay alive flashed through my mind.

The Soviets were desperate for manpower, and wasted no time with further examinations. I was promptly inducted into the Russian army, hoping to rejoin my friend, Aaron.

It was a futile hope. I saw Aaron only once, just before he was sent to the front lines. Since I never heard from Aaron again, I assumed that my good friend had been killed.

Now survival took a new twist. Just three weeks after boot

camp, the new recruits were ordered to the front. We barely knew how to shoot a gun or how to perform any infantryman's duties in the field. As far as I was concerned, I was good only for an easy German target, a bitter and ironic situation.

Several thousand Russian soldiers boarded a train heading west, to provide reinforcements for a battered division of the army. The day we departed from Samarkand, my bunk was next to that of a young corporal whose girlfriend had brought him a bottle of cologne as a going-away present. The corporal drank the cologne and became very sick. Every time the train bumped, he retched all over both of us.

After two weeks on the crowded train, we arrived in Moscow, where we were given steam baths, and our clothes were disinfected. Army rations were insufficient, and we were constantly hungry. Another week on the train brought us within 100 miles of the German-Russian battlefront. I was sent to the infantry division.

The new reinforcements were processed by the company commander, a young Ukrainian lieutenant, who asked a number of questions.

"Your background, please?"

"Polish citizen from Skoczow," I answered when my turn came.

"Education?"

"High school diploma," a small lie I thought to say. I had dropped out my last year to work in Berman's flour mill.

"Family?"

"Polish Jews." I learned later that Russian soldiers were in the habit of deserting the army when they approached their own villages, and were, therefore, under tighter scrutiny than non-nationals.

"Since you have a high school education, you will be in my communication service. You are assigned to my company," the lieutenant informed me at the end of the interrogation.

The lie about my educational diploma had dubiously

"qualified" me to be the batman for the company commander, a first lieutenant, and three second lieutenants. While the company was billeted in a confiscated farm house, I cleaned the officers' boots, brought their food, ran errands, and cleaned their quarters. Another duty in the "communication service" was to accompany the commander into the villages whenever the officer visited the ladies, in case a military emergency should occur at a time when the lieutenant was indisposed. I wished to be relieved of this "honorable" position as soon as possible.

During the war games, I was assigned to stand guard at an imaginary bridge. The platoon marched off with their lieutenant, and I was left standing alone in a barren field of snow. Before long, my hands and feet were numb and stiff, and I had seen a good many cases of frostbite already, a common affliction here. After all the miseries I had so far survived, the present situation seemed an absurdity. I suddenly decided that I was not going to freeze to death senselessly in a Russian war game. I went back to the hut to get warm and dry, and fell asleep on the huge stove that divided the room. An hour later, I heard the soldiers returning from their field exercises. It was too late to get back to the post. I was caught off guard duty, a serious offense in any army. The lieutenant was furious.

"Why did you leave your post, Urbach?"

"I thought I was freezing, sir. My hands and feet were numb."

"That's no excuse! You know the penalty for leaving your post. We will hold a court martial hearing tonight. Be there at seven, sharp!"

That night, I was sentenced to three days of solitary confinement. A corporal with a rifle and bayonet escorted me to battalion headquarters, about five miles down the road.

"They really did you in, Urbach," the corporal sympathized. "Do you know where you have to spend those three days? In an unheated barn, and they don't give you any hot food either. You'll be lucky if you don't freeze to death there."

"Three days are nothing," I scoffed. "I spent more than a year in prison in Siberia. I'm an old hand at this kind of treatment. Besides, three miserable days, I'm out, and no more a batman! I'll be happy to give up such a privilege."

About a month later, I was transferred to a unit of engineers closer to the front. In the platoon, a Communist agitator politicked for membership in the young Communist party organization. Thinking this might be an opportunity to get out of the infantry unit, I joined the meetings for indoctrination. At the completion of the course, a captain from division headquarters came to initiate the new members into the party. Captain Singerman was a small, red-haired Jew from Odessa. After the ceremony, I introduced myself with an idea in mind that I hoped would provide a more substantial reason to be withdrawn from the infantry.

"Captain Singerman, I'm languishing here. I know there is a war to be fought, but I have something more useful to the army than just carrying a rifle. We are fighting Germans, right? I am fluent in their language. We do get P.O.W.'s, don't we?"

"Yes, we do. What do you have in mind?"

"How about my being of some kind of help to you with the German prisoners?"

"I'll think about it," Singerman replied, his eyes narrowing with interest.

Singerman thought fast. That same evening, he informed the lieutenant that I was going to accompany him to division headquarters for an interview. The two of us walked for nearly three hours, during which time there was not much talk between us. Singerman was not going to commit himself prematurely, and avoided getting into friendly conversation. Finally, we came to another billet in a peasant family's house, and Singerman took me inside.

"Wait here," he ordered. "Someone will come to see you soon."

Thirty minutes later, a young officer appeared, nicely

dressed in a crisp, tailored-to-fit uniform, and hat to match.

"Ata medaber evrit?" (Do you speak Hebrew?)

"Ken. Ani medaber evrit." (Yes, I speak Hebrew).

"Do you speak English?"

"Yes. I speak English.

"Sprechen Sie deutsch?"

"Jawohl. Ich spreche deutsch."

The officer then introduced himself.

"My name is Lt. Misha Rabinovich. I'm from Vilna" [now Soviet Lithuania]. "Sorry for the grill. I was told to find out what languages you know."

"So why have you brought me here? Is there a chance that I could be an interpreter?"

"A good chance, I think. But you'll have to wait until the division moves forward to the front to engage and capture German prisoners."

"I understand, Lieutenant. Too bad for the wait. I hope it won't be too long. I don't like the odds out there on the front line."

I was sent back to my division after the interview, and continued to be trained for combat. With the Pioneer Battalion, I also labored at building bridges, roads, and passages through marshes. We slept in the forest, and worked our way toward the front lines. The army was preparing for a big offensive.

Within 100 yards of the German trenches, the battalion worked at night, crossing a ravine in the forest to build machine gun enclosures and deepen the Russian trenches. Once every hour, the Germans fired mortar rounds at us, inflicting many casualties. A soldier near me had his head blown off. I took the boots off the dead soldier since mine were worn out, and my comrade would not be needing them any more.

On June 22, 1944, the offensive began. That same day, I was summoned by an officer's messenger.

"Urbach, get your gear together. You are going with me."

"Why? What have I done?"

"Nothing. I have orders to take you to battalion headquarters, that's all I know."

At battalion headquarters, I was delivered to Captain Wolfson, a Jew from Leningrad.

"Yes, sir. Sgt. Urbach reporting."

"I'm sending you back to our main headquarters today. They need a translator there. The big push is on, and we'll be picking up German prisoners any time now. Go get your papers and some food from the sergeant. You are to leave at once."

"Thank you very much, sir." I saluted sharply. "I'll be on my way within the hour."

On foot by myself, I began the 20-mile walk eastward, back to the main headquarters. From a distance, I witnessed a full-scale fire barrage between the Germans and the Russians. The artillery and katyusha rocket exchange was an awesome scene I would never forget. If I had not been called away suddenly, I would have participated in that battle. It was reported later that eighty percent of the soldiers in my battalion were killed in that engagement. When the casualty figures appeared, I praised the God I did not yet know for sparing me again, and thought of home folks, particularly of Mama, who must be praying for me—she always did that. At that moment, I had a strong awareness of my mother's near presence. The feeling was so powerful, I was moved to address her personally.

"Mama, I know you are alive somewhere. Thank you for your prayers. I think God listens to you. He does seem to be protecting me."

ॐ

The Soviets broke through the German lines and drove their main army into retreat. Remnants of the German army were encircled in the forest, leaving pockets of enemy resistance to be routed out or killed. I was assigned to assist a colonel in planting twenty-five German prisoners of war inside the enemy enclaves to spread unrest and dissension. The P.O.W.'s selected for this mission were non-German nationals who were forced to

serve in Hitler's army. They were given a two-week indoctrination course in an "anti-Fascist school," and then ordered to
infiltrate the German lines. Using the propaganda techniques
they were taught in the indoctrination course, the P.O.W.'s were
to encourage the entrapped Germans to surrender to the
Russians. Although the main bait was to tell the Germans that
they had the choice of being a live prisoner of war or a dead
soldier, many were shot by the Russians when they surrendered.

Following the route of the Nazi retreat from White Russia,
the colonel and I transported the newly-trained P.O.W.'s in an
open truck. We drove 400 miles, passing abandoned guns and
stores of ammunition, destroyed tanks, naked and bloated dead
German soldiers (the Russians took their boots, clothing, and
other valuables), and dead horses with swollen bellies covered
with flies. The scenes of the ravages of war were sickening and
unforgettable.

I was airborne for my next assignment.

"Have you ever been in an airplane before?" my command-
ing officer asked.

"No, sir, but I'm willing to go up. What is the mission?" I
was certainly ready for something to blot out the recent
experience on the ground.

"Good. We need you aboard a small plane scheduled to fly
over the German remnants in the forest. The plane is equipped
with a loudspeaker. You will tell the Germans in their own
language that their only hope is to surrender. Do you understand?"

"Yes, sir. I can certainly do that."

Many Germans heeded the warning, and surrendered to the
Russians. It was an assignment I did not mind doing at all.

The Soviets entered Poland in the summer of 1944. I was
sent to work for the Russian newspaper in Novogrudok, a town
in northern Poland. The newspaper was printed in a sidelined
train. My job included editing, proofreading, and some writing. A

Jewish man named Shapiro was typesetter for the newspaper.

"The Nazis killed my whole family in the Grodno ghetto," he told me. "I was out at the time they came, or they would have gotten me, too. After that, I spent two years in the forests around Bialystok, fighting with the Polish guerrillas against the Germans. You know, Bialystok once had a large Jewish population. Now most of the Jews are dead."

Being the only Jew in my army unit, I had little contact with other Jews, and was unaware of the terrible events in Poland. Now on native soil again, Shapiro's story was soon followed by another, and another. It was then that I had a premonition that my own family had been killed.

In 1939, there were about ten million Jews in Europe. By 1945, the Nazis had killed over five million, and another million Jews probably died from disease and starvation. Before the war, large and virile Jewish communities existed in some 2000 cities and villages in Poland. Hitler located most of his extermination camps in that country, making Poland a Jewish graveyard. In August, 1945, Jews were found in only 224 places in the country. Almost ninety percent of the Jewish communities had been completely obliterated from the map. Of Poland's 3,300,000 Jews, an estimated 2,800,000 had perished by 1945. More than half of the victims were killed at a camp near Lublin in southeast Poland. After the war, many Jews remained in displaced persons, "DP," camps. In 1983, less than 7000 Jews were left in Poland.

Shapiro put me in touch with other Jews who had survived in the surrounding towns, villages, ghettos, and forests, hiding from the Poles and Ukrainians as well as the Germans. There was a price on Jewish heads, and the local people turned the refugees in for the reward.

In September, the two of us went to a Rosh Hashanah service at a Jewish home. It was a devastating, tragic day. The survivors of the Holocaust wept as they recited the New Year prayers, and mourned the fate that had befallen their families. Each person at the service had a terrible, deeply-distressing story to tell. The testimonies of so many grief stricken people heard all at once, seared my mind and broke my heart. I was not yet twenty-three years old, and felt bereft of everything that made life reasonable and normal. How could anybody feel normal after living through the insane destruction that had engulfed so many millions of people?

❦

During my seven-year odyssey to freedom, I saw a variety of reactions to the Holocaust. Some Jews, like those who attended the Rosh Hashanah service, clung to faith, but were bewildered at God's silence during Hitler's evil reign of death. Others, particularly young Jews, became atheists, losing faith altogether, and gave themselves over to anger and hatred. Still others fell into a limbo of neither here nor there, unable to deny God's existence completely, but left with a faith too devitalized to restore their broken spirits.

"Where was God when the six million died?" The question will continue to be asked. For many Jewish people, the belief in an omnipotent, beneficient God became impossible after Auschwitz.

Jewish history records other calculated attempts to exterminate the Jews, which were ultimately woven into national celebrations of victory over the enemies of God's chosen people. Passover celebrates the miraculous deliverance from Pharaoh of Egypt. Purim is the annual festival in memory of the defeat of Haman's plot to annihilate all the Jews in the Persian Empire. Hanukkah remembers the victory over Antiochus Epiphanes of Syria during the Maccabean period. But none of the genocidal schemes of the past compare with the diabolical sadism and demented brutality of Hitler's death camps. It would seem blasphemous and obscene to look for any meaningful expression of God's purposes in the Holocaust experience.

In time, I would be led to look for the answer to the question not so much in God's heart, but in the hearts of men. As I studied the Scriptures several years later, I learned that my forefathers consistently discerned a flaw in human nature.

Isaiah observed a "rebellious people, who walk in a way that is not good, following their own desires . . ." (Isaiah 65:2). The Psalmist wrote despairingly: "They (the children of men) have all gone astray, they are all alike corrupt; there is none that does good, no, not one." (Psalm 14:3). Jeremiah lamented: "The heart is deceitful above all things, and desperately corrupt; who can understand it?" (Jeremiah 17:9)

I began to ask myself, "Can we really blame God for human evil-doing?" From the religious history of mankind, and from my own personal experience, I came to realize that God will not coerce love and obedience from the people He created free to choose for or against His revealed will.

Is not the real question vis-a-vis the Holocaust: "Where was humanity when God "has showed you O man, what is good; and what does the Lord require of you but to do justice, and to love kindness, and to walk humbly with your God?" (Micah 6:8)

I worked my way slowly through the question that haunts every Jewish mind, and all morally sensitive people. I concluded that if I must try to understand the Third Reich horror in terms of good and evil, then I must do so from the biblical perspective on corporate human sinfulness. We are all caught up in a cosmic spiritual warfare. The only victory over such evil surely must await the coming of the Messiah, as my forefathers prophesied and hoped for. What the Jewish prophets did not anticipate was that the Messiah would come to save us one by one for a specified period of time—"until the times of the Gentiles are fulfilled." When the world's cup of iniquity is full, then He will come again, "to judge the earth . . . and the peoples with his truth." (Psalm 96:13). In that day, "They shall not hurt or destroy in all my holy mountain; for the earth shall be full of the knowledge of the Lord as the waters cover the sea." (Isaiah 11:9). Meanwhile, we are summoned by God to continue to love even in a world where love has grown cold.

This understanding of the spiritual causes of evil came

much later in my life. Beyond the Rosh Hashanah service, I still had much to suffer, and would experience more godlessness before I made the connection between humanity's failure and God's response to it.

⟡

With no discernible future, and feeling certain that my family was dead, I abandoned myself to recklessness and despair. When the war ended with Germany's unconditional surrender on May 7, 1945, I joined the Russians in celebrating the victory by drinking and dancing at a party. A Russian officer who had imbibed too much alcohol, grabbed me by the arm and towed me away from my dancing partner. The Russian pulled out his revolver and pointed it in my face.

"Listen, you, I like your partner. Leave her for me, or I'll shoot you right now!"

"Have your pick, and leave me alone," I quickly obliged.

Even with this preview, I was horrified later when the Russians, in a drunken frenzy, began to shoot people, rape, and rob. "Peace" looked very much like war.

At a party in Bromberg, a frivolous remark, made with no malicious intent, resulted in more trouble and changed the course of my life.

"Did you know," I said to a small group of friends, "while our superior officers are eating and drinking and having a merry time, Lt. Rosenstein and Sgt. Urbach, two Jews, are putting out the newspaper!"

The comment was overheard and reported to the Polish colonel in the Russian army, and I was summoned to Colonel Sawitzky's headquarters.

"Yes, sir?" I reported crisply, unaware of the reason for the summons.

"I've heard that you shot off your mouth and spread some uncomplimentary information about your superior officers, Sgt. Urbach. There is no call for you to say such things. We must make an example of you. A court martial is in order . . . here are your papers. You are to go to the front headquarters in Stettin, and I'm sending my batman, Kostia, with you. The man is a thief, and I'm tired of bailing him out of trouble. He will be joining you in court martial proceedings, and we will be well rid of both of you. You will leave immediately."

The colonel terminated the interview without giving me time to reply to the charge, which would have been futile anyway.

Kostia and I were soon on the train for the long trip to Stettin. Enroute, we ate at a restaurant in Bydgoszcz. During the meal, I reviewed the situation in my own mind. I was tired of being buffeted about on the circumstantial authority of foreigners who did not care whether I lived or died. I decided that it was time to take my fate into my own hands.

"Kostia, I'm not going to Stettin. You go your way, and I'll go mine. This is my country and I can swim in it quite well."

Kostia grimaced in disapproval.

"What do you mean you're not going to Stettin? We have orders to go to Stettin. What is to become of me if you desert? I have no money and no place to go. You are no better off than I am. Why don't you want to go with me?"

"Kostia, don't be naive. I know very well what is going to happen in Stettin. The military will make an example of us in another one of their 'show trials.' A number of things could be done with us, all unpleasant and unnecessary. We could be sentenced to a year or two in prison, sent back to Russia to working battalion, or who knows what else they could think up as punishment. No, thanks, Kostia. Stettin is bad news. Good luck and goodbye!"

I boarded the night train to Lodz. Along the way, I threw my documents, army uniform, and gun out of the train window. I donned a civilian shirt, jacket, and cap, which I had brought with me. German army pants and Russian boots completed my non-descript outfit. Parts of army uniforms were worn by many civilians, so I was not conspicuously dressed. When I arrived in

Lodz, I was a different man.

ᴥ

The election to go to the city of Lodz was related to an incident that occurred shortly after my return to Poland with the Russian army. While working on the newspaper in Novogrudok, I encountered some young Jewish guerrillas who survived the war in forests and mountains. They were bitter with the Poles for anti-Semitism in the country, and equally disdained the Germans and Russians. They were friendly at the time, but taunted me repeatedly.

"Why are you still wearing those Russian rags! Be a man! Get out before they stand you against a wall. Leave the army and come with us now!"

Their vagabond life did not appeal to me then. My job offered some security, decent food, and the freedom to socialize when I was not working on the newspaper. Things could be worse, and worse was relative to my previous experience in prison.

"No, thanks, comrades," I declined. "I'm not ready to be a gypsy."

"Well, just in case you change your mind, here is our address in Lodz. Look for our hang-out if you're ever in town. We keep busy."

The group did not tell me what kind of activities they were inviting me to join.

ᴥ

An industrial city located in central Poland, and the second largest city in the country, Lodz once had a Jewish population of 100,000. The Nazis destroyed nearly all of the Jews there during their occupation of Poland. I had no reason to choose any particular destination except in the haphazard course of events, one was suggested to me. Afloat and alone once again, I went to Lodz. I looked up the youth gang whose address I had kept, but did not stay long in their company because their way of life was appallingly brutal. They were still guerrillas, five boys and a girl, who crossed the border to Germany, entered homes, stole goods, and even killed people. They brought back loot which they sold on the black market.

Discouraged and lonely, I walked along a street in Lodz, pondering what to do next. Suddenly, I saw a familiar face in the crowd.

"Wolicki!!" I called out, and approached the man. "Eliezer Urbach here. It's been a long time. I thought you might not recognize me. What are you doing here in Lodz?"

The man was a Polish army officer whom I knew before the war. He was married to a Jewish lady, and was a newspaper man in Skoczow. Now he was a correspondent for a newspaper in Lublin on assignment in Lodz.

"I might ask you the same question! Delighted to see you, Urbach! How about some coffee and talk?"

Wolicki and I went into the nearest coffee house, where we reminisced and exchanged stories of wartime events. However, I did not tell him that I had deserted the Russian army. Having had enough of Russian prisons, I was not ready to trust anyone with such information.

"I need a job, Wolicki. Do you have any good ideas?"

"I might," Wolicki replied thoughtfully. "You said you did newspaper work during the war. Would you like to continue in that line?"

"Yes, I would feel experienced at that."

"In that case, I think I know just the right place for you. A government paper is being published in Lublin. I'll send a recommendation with you, and I'm pretty sure they'll take you on. By the way, do you have any identification papers?"

"As a matter of fact, I don't."

"Then you had better get some before going to Lublin. There is a Jewish Committee here in Lodz that issues new papers for Jewish refugees, and they don't ask any questions. Here's the address. I suggest you take care of this right now."

"Thank you very much, Wolicki. I appreciate all your help.

I'll leave tomorrow."

"Fine. Meet me back at this coffee house at 5 o'clock this evening and I'll take you home with me. You can stay with us tonight. My wife will be glad to see you, too."

Under my real name, I would now be on record as a Russian army deserter, and likely be soon arrested. I secured papers from the Jewish Committee under an uncle's name, Henry Fabiszkiewicz, having to state only my age and birthplace along with the name. The following morning, I left by train for Lublin, about 150 miles from Lodz. With Wolicki's letter of recommendation, I was hired as a night editor at the newspaper office, and worked there for several months.

However, I was not content in Lublin. The fate of my parents was continually on my mind. I had to know if they were alive or dead. Unable to rest with the uncertainty, I quit the job in the Fall of 1945, and set out for the town of my birth.

[Editor's note. The camaraderie among Jews has provoked a conspiracy phobia in nearly every country in the world at one time or another. The consistent manner in which Jewish people care for their own engenders profound envy and hostility, where it does not elicit admiration. When cloaked with unjustified political implications, the extraordinary charity characteristic of all Jewish communities gives rise to the irrational fear of a "Zionist conspiracy," as well as to the accusation that "Jews only care for their own." Both the fear and the accusation are false. The proverbial generosity of Jews, to other Jews and non-Jews alike, is the fulfillment of biblical and rabbinical commandments incumbent upon all. At a time when all Jewish lives in Hitler's Europe were threatened, Eliezer always knew he could turn to his own brethren for help and support. Within the story of his escape from the Nazis and long odyssey to freedom, the code of Jewish brotherhood is remarkably apparent.]

CHAPTER 8

Home Again

I was born December 7, 1921, in Skoczow, Poland, a town of about 6000 citizens, in the district Cieszyn. Located in the picturesque Carpathian mountains on the Vistula River, Cieszyn was separated from Czechoslovakia by the Olza River. Like many Jews, the Urbach family lived a simple, rural life. I loved the land, and enjoyed taking care of our vegetable garden when I was a young boy.

Arriving at 218 Bielska Street, the house where I was born, I did not find my parents there. Instead, residing in our home were the town dogcatcher, his wife, and nine children. Two of the daughters had children by German soldiers. I introduced myself, and asked the dogcatcher for information concerning my parents.

"I think you should go talk to your former nanny, Helena," the man suggested. "She is living on some land your father gave to her. She stayed with your parents until the end, and she was spared by the Nazis."

I knew the location of my father's land, and needed no directions to find Helena. The reunion with her was a mixture of joy and grief.

"Eliezer!" Helena cried out, when she opened the door at

my knocking. "Thank God you are alive! I can hardly believe my eyes! Is it really you? Bless God! I have prayed for you every day since you left! Come in! Come into the house!"

Helena's eyes were brimming with tears as she rushed to embrace my thin frame. She ushered me into house, buoying me almost off the floor in her strong arms. Although she knew what had to be foremost in my mind, Helena kept me busy answering a flood of questions about my own whereabouts for six years. I myself was dreading the moment when the reason for coming home had to be faced. Telling Helena about Ernest's death was hard enough. We both wept until Helena brought our emotions under control with a prayer for the repose of Ernest's soul.

"Helena, tell me about my parents. What happened to them?" I finally found the strength to ask.

Helena took my hands into her own, and gripped them tightly. I had been gone a long time, but I was still very young, a boy yet to Helena. She knew my fears about my family, but it was agonizing for her to confirm the actual facts.

"In 1943, your father and mother, along with three other families who had been forced to live in their house, were taken away by the Germans and never returned. They had been permitted to stay alive until the very end. Even though your father was over eighty years old when they came to get him, he put up a fight. The soldiers tied him hand and foot, and took him on a lorry to Auschwitz."

Auschwitz was just 30 miles from Skoczow.

By this time, I was too numb with grief to weep. A feeling of disconsolate loneliness came over me, and I stared at the floor with glassy, non-seeing eyes. Helena, who had helped raise me and my brother while our mother was busy with the restaurant and inn, moved to bring me back to the present.

"Eliezer, dear," she said quietly but firmly, "you must stay here with me for a while, until you get your bearings, or as long as you want. Take my bedroom, and I will manage just fine elsewhere."

"Helena, you are too kind. I don't see any other bed in the house, and the floor is no place for you. I won't let you make me comfortable at your own expense!"

"Nonsense! You do as I say for once!" Helena insisted, and smiled as she alluded to my former willfulness.

She would not be persuaded otherwise, and her compassion prevailed. During my stay with Helena, I questioned her about the fate of other people in Skoczow.

"What happened to my friends—Franciszek Kubaczka, Jozef Pieter, Novak, Skiba, and the others?"

"Most of your Gentile friends were conscripted into the German army," Helena told me. "If they refused to go, they were sent to concentration camps or killed. Some are still prisoners of war, captured during the Russian invasion. Others are missing in action. Two or three made it back with the Polish army that the Russians mobilized somewhere. There are very few left here for you to contact, and I'm not sure what these are finding to do."

I discovered for myself what some of my old friends were doing. Former **Sila** members had re-established the organization under the new designation, Polish Workers' Party. They were a Communist-front organization, and were harassed and hunted by the Polish anti-Communist underground.

A battle was now raging in Poland between the old regime and the Communists. The old regime was a Polish government-in-exile established in London after the German and Russian division of Poland in 1939. The Russian army invaded German-controlled Poland in 1944. A Russian-dominated government was set up in Lublin in opposition to the Polish government in London. In January, 1945, Russia recognized the Lublin Committee as the provisional government of Poland. A month later, at the Yalta Conference, the United States and Great Britain also agreed to recognize the Communist-dominated Lublin group as the new provisional government. The Communists crushed all resistance in 1945.

I did not rejoin the ex-**Sila** group, but socialized with my few former friends and kept aware of dangerous political undercurrents. With the testimony of the former police commissioner, Heiman Urbach's friend, and Helena as the second witness, I established my identity as Papa's sole heir, and took possession of the house, inn, and surrounding fields. I tried to stay in Skoczow, but the tormenting thoughts of my parents' fate gave me no peace. Marriage and family life in Poland were unthinkable. My social life was superficial and unsatisfying. I lived in a state of numb shock, feeling nothing, and totally disinterested in any permanent alliances.

One day, attending the funeral of a Communist party official who had been killed by the Polish underground, I saw a Jewish face.

"Yankel! What are you doing here?"

The introductory address, "Yankel," established the Jewishness of both of us. The man was a policeman by the name of Pomeranz, who had survived Auschwitz. Pomeranz had an indelible number on his arm. With Jewish camaraderie activated, we fell easily into conversation of a personal nature.

"I understand your misery here," Pomeranz sympathized. "You have too many painful memories to deal with. You need a change of scenery. Come and stay with me in Cieszyn. You'll find a lot of Jewish survivors there. New friends, new faces will do you good. How about it?"

"Maybe you're right, Pomeranz. I'm wasting away here. All right, I'll come for a while and see how it goes."

"That's just great!" Pomeranz smiled, sealing the new friendship with a handshake. "I guarantee that you'll find life in Cieszyn more interesting than here in Skoczow."

Pomeranz did not add that he had a use for my border pass into Czechoslovakia. In the course of our conversation, I had told him the story of how I came to have the permanent pass that allowed me to move freely back and forth across the border. For the privilege of being the son of Heiman Urbach, who was known and highly respected by the Czech officials, I was issued the pass with no questions asked.

Amenable to any diversion, I went to Cieszyn, a city of 20,000 people, just fifteen kilometers from Skoczow. I soon learned that Pomeranz was involved in smuggling Jewish people, mostly Polish army deserters, across the border into Czechoslovakia on their way to the free world. For a short while, I found the excitement a welcome relief from depression. One night, as we were leaving Pomeranz's apartment, we were met by police.

"Halt! You are under arrest!"

"What for?" Pomeranz asked in mock innocence.

"You know very well what for!" one of the policemen retorted angrily. "How do you think we found you? We have a good source of information, and we know you are smuggling. Now don't give us any trouble, and come along quickly!"

Pomeranz and I were thrown into a temporary prison, which, ironically, was the cellar of the high school I attended in Cieszyn before the war. About one hundred other men were incarcerated in the prison, most of whom had been arrested for political rather than criminal offenses. Even a jest against the Communist government could be punished by five or six years in prison. The city commandant was a Russian colonel.

The two of us were separated and interrogated continuously all night. We both denied the smuggling charge. I did not reveal to the Russians that I spoke their language, for fear it might lead to the discovery that I had deserted the Russian army.

Several days later, I was aroused at 1:00 a.m. by a Polish policeman who thrust a piece of paper in my face.

"Do you know what this is, Urbach?" the man asked menacingly.

"I have no idea."

"Your friend Pomeranz has signed a written confession to the crime of smuggling people out of Poland. Now what do you say?"

"Pomeranz's confession doesn't make me guilty."

"We've got you both so don't give me any smart answers! Three people you transported illegally out of the country have been caught, and they informed on you. There is no doubt about your activities."

Imprisoned for another unknown period of time awaiting trial, one of my duties was peeling potatoes. Constantly hungry, I stole a few potatoes and hid them in my shirt, but a suspicious guard searched me. A merciless beating followed the attempted theft. I was close to preferring a death sentence rather than spend one more minute in prison.

My despair was soon relieved. The Polish police came to me with a proposition that would gain my release from prison.

"You're stuck now, Urbach. What can you do? You are guilty of a serious offense and will have to pay. There will be a trial, and you'll be behind bars a few years. Unless, of course, you would like to cooperate with us?"

"How do you mean 'cooperate?' "

"You were born and raised here. You are familiar with the territory and move around freely among the people. You hear what is going on, and we know there is a large smuggling operation in existence—deserters, American money, saccharin—are going over the border. We need someone who can provide us with good information about these activities."

"In other words, you want an informer."

"If you want to call it that, yes."

"Well, I can't help you behind these bars."

"We'll take care of that. You only have to sign a few vouchers for our protection."

I was now an expert at seizing opportunities to be free. That very evening, after only two weeks in prison, I was released on the promise that I would spy for the police—a promise I had no intention of keeping. The Russian colonel suspected I was lying, and made a dire threat.

"Go, but if you run away, I'll squeeze the life out of you!"

"I know what's good for me," I assured him, privately

amused at my double-talk answer. I never expected to see the colonel again for any reason.

It was Friday night at 9 o'clock when I left the prison. As I walked the fifteen kilometers back to Skoczow, I prayed a small prayer to remote Deity, the usual mixture of superstition and gratitude. Three hours later, I arrived at Helena's house.

"Where have you been, Eliezer? I've been so anxious for you."

"In prison again."

"I had a feeling that was where you might be. In fact, I dreamed the same. What are you going to do now?"

"I was released to spy for the Polish police, and the first report is due Monday morning. But you know I can't do such a thing. I have to leave Poland. My Uncle Henry Fabiszkiewicz is in Munich. I'm going there now."

Helena was chagrined at the thought of my leaving again, particularly under such threatening circumstances, but she knew I had no choice.

"Will this world ever return to sanity?" she sighed in reluctant resignation to my departure. "Must you always be running from soldiers, police, and prisons? You might never get back home again after this. You'll never be safe here anymore. Well, everything is out of our hands right now. I know you must be out of the country by Monday. I'll pack some food for you. Eliezer, in the future, please don't get involved in political activities. Don't invite trouble that way. I'll pray to God for your safety every day, and will write to you whenever it's possible for a letter to reach you. Go with God, my son."

Saturday, I rented the house and fields to a butcher, who gave me 10,000 German marks for two years in advance. The money was not valid Polish currency, but I hoped to be able to use it in Germany. I put the banknotes in my boots under my longjohns and knickers. That night, I took a circuitous northern route on foot through the mountains to cross the border into Czechoslovakia. On Sunday, I doubled back south to the Czech side of

Cieszyn to collect several thousand Czech korunas that I had left
with my cousin, Toni, who survived the war in a workers'
camp.

"Do we know anybody in Moravska Ostrava?" I asked
Toni.

"Yes, the boys are there." (The boys were Jewish friends
who survived concentration camps.) "Here are addresses where
you can find them. Good luck, Eliezer. I hope you get to Germany
safely. Give my regards to Uncle Henry."

From Cieszyn, I took a train to Moravska Ostrava, where I
picked up the names and addresses of more Jewish survivors in
Karlsbad. At Karlsbad, I rented a flatbed truck and offered to take
thirty-five Jewish refugees across the border. Five check-points
were on the route, three Russian and two American. The Russian
check-points were no problem. The guards were easily bribed
with vodka and cigarettes.

Most of the refugees already had papers to get through the
American check-points. A few others besides myself did not, and
the truck was stopped. The Americans were well-supplied with
cigarettes and vodka, and did their duty.

"Sorry, you people without papers. We can't let you through.
You'll have to get off the truck here," the American soldier
ordered.

"We understand, sir," I responded for the group. "We're not
really law-breakers, only refugees."

I spoke a few words to the driver of the truck, and waved
him off. The American soldiers paid no attention to those of us
on foot who struck off into the forest. It was a short detour. We
simply walked around the check-point and met the truck again
about a mile up the road.

My destination was the city of Munich, capital of Bavaria,
where Hitler rose to power, and now one of the centers for the
American occupation of Germany. I found my uncle and second
wife, a Russian lady, living in a railroad car. Because of a family
obligation, and as a destitute survivor of the Holocaust, I

expected Uncle Henry to help me.

My mother, Berta Urbach, had helped both of her brothers, Henry and Isadore, through hard times. After her marriage to my father, a prosperous man, she became the family benefactress. Henry served as an officer in the Austrian army during World War I, been wounded and taken prisoner of war. Set free, he was later drafted into the Polish army, where he became an officer and was captured by the Russians. When he returned from the war, he was on crutches and suffering from arthritis. He came to live with the newly married Urbachs in Skoczow, and recuperated with the fresh air and good food there. He never forgot the kindness.

Henry's first wife was killed in Auschwitz. While he was in the concentration camp, the Nazis broke Henry's elbow and knocked out his teeth. A nephew, who was a skilled engineer, secured false Aryan papers to make his own escape, and was working in Kiev. By courier, he sent Russian gold coins sown into a book to the camp for his uncle. The gold bought Henry his freedom, and he went to Kiev to join his nephew, who obtained false Aryan papers also for Henry. In Kiev, Henry met his second wife, Luba, a practicing engineer. Her first husband, a member of the Russian intelligentsia, was executed in the purges of 1935. Luba was left with a child, and spent several years in exile and prison. Henry and Luba together had barely escaped death a number of times.

Somehow, I had expected my uncle's circumstances to be more favorable.

"German money has been devalued," Henry explained. "My salary doesn't go very far. The German economy is severely depressed. There is no living to be made here. The fact is, Eliezer, we have been thinking about emigrating to Brazil. Maybe you can help us do that. Meanwhile, we will rent a flat with more space, and you must find a job."

The three of us rented a small apartment, and I obtained a job with UNRRA, the United Nations Relief and Rehabilitation

Agency. However, living with my relatives was not a happy arrangement. Frequent arguments with my aunt and uncle over my activities kept us all on edge.

"Eliezer, you are out almost every night jeopardizing your safety. Post-war Munich is a dreadful city, full of thugs, thieves, murderers, drunken soldiers, and other criminal elements. No one is safe on the streets at night. We do not approve of your gallivanting around so much and being such a worry to us. Please stay home at night and give us some peace!"

"Aunt Luba," I protested, "I can take care of myself. Please don't get so upset. There are lots of people like myself who just want to be sociable and forget the war. We all like to go to parties, dance, and have a good time. Let me alone to do as I please. I don't like to fight with you and Uncle Henry."

"Then stay home and stop causing the trouble!"

The arguments continued until I moved out of the flat to ease the strain on our relationship.

✿

As a guard at the UNRRA base, I met many other DP's—Russians, Ukrainians, Poles, Greeks, Jews, and White Russians. They were exciting companions. Many of them were nobility, White Russian noblesse who had escaped to Bulgaria and Hungary until the Soviets caught up with them. Princes and barons worked as waiters and guards. There were many runaway Russian soldiers, famous musicians, and Yugoslavians who had fled after King Peter was defeated. The atmosphere was convivial, and I enjoyed having very interesting friends.

Eventually, I was transferred to a different UNRRA billet in Munich. There I met Captain Wolkowicz, a Jewish lawyer from Lodz. Once an army officer during the war (British or American army, I was never sure which), Wolkowicz now worked for UNRRA. A handsome man of medium stature, and piercing black eyes, Wolkowicz exuded self-confidence and worldly poise.

"I'll be on my way to Belgium soon," he told me. "I lived

there before the war, and my wife and two children are in Brussels."

"Is that right? I'd like to settle down, too, in Palestine, I've decided. Looks like that's the best place for Jews."

"If you are serious, I can provide you with the necessary documents to go to Palestine," Wolkowicz volunteered.

"I am serious, and that would be a great help. I understand that getting to Palestine is no snap achievement. I'll be in touch."

Wolkowicz was the first Jew that I had ever met who said he had converted to Christianity. He had married a Gentile woman and "converted" for the sake of convenience. However, I could see that Wolkowicz' confessed religion made no difference in his life. He was, in fact, quite a bon vivant, sleeping with the hotel maids and other German women whose husbands were killed in Russia. He was a crass drunkard, and talked incessantly about his sexual conquests. Wolkowicz had money, food, and wine, and invited me to one of his lavish parties.

"This man lives it up like the goyim," I thought to myself. I did not approve of Wolkowicz' way of life, but I had learned not to question providential contacts that led to open doors. I had not been searching for anything in particular, just moving randomly with the tide of displaced humanity. My decision to go to Palestine represented my first long-range plan to start a new life.

Bored with life in Germany and restless in spirit, I soon pressed Wolkowicz to make good on the offer to help me get to Palestine.

"All right, if you're so eager to go. Get yourself a British uniform somewhere," Wolkowicz instructed. "I'll take care of the rest. Tomorrow we're going to Paris, and then on to Brussels."

A recent incident laid the most promising groundwork for fulfilling Wolkowicz' instructions. A Polish truck driver for a Catholic charity organization affiliated with UNRRA was attracted to a watch I wore.

"Where did you get the fancy watch?"

"I took it off a dead German officer during the war. It's a very good watch."

"I can see that. Would you like to sell it to me? I'll give you a good price for it."

"No, thanks, Yuzek. I doubt if I come by another watch like this one. I think I'll hang on to it."

As I left the meeting with Wolkowicz, I spotted Yuzek in his truck, and hailed him.

"Hey! Yuzek! Pull up for a minute!"

"Sure. What's up?"

"Are you still interested in my watch? If so, I'll make a bargain with you."

"You bet! What's the bargain?"

"The watch for a complete British army uniform. Can you do it?"

"No problem. It's a deal!"

Yuzek acquired the uniform, and I reported to Wolkowicz that I was ready to go.

"You have the uniform already? You sure didn't waste any time."

"Indeed, I have it!" I assured him.

"Very well, then. Tonight, an UNRRA truck will leave from the billet at 6:00 p.m. Be there on time, and wear the uniform smartly. I'll be on the truck, but you don't know me, understand? If we have to talk, you answer me in monosyllables. It's best we don't appear too well-acquainted. I've made unauthorized use of UNRRA letterhead stationery, so we could both get into trouble with this venture. But I'd like to see you make it out of Germany safely. Good luck!"

That evening as scheduled, a G.M.C. tarpaulin-covered UNRRA truck arrived at the billet. I appeared in the British army uniform with round red UNRRA insignia on the sleeve, and climbed aboard. With my best English, I merely wished the other passengers a good evening, and spoke no more. The truck was stopped at the gate.

"Where are you going, sir?" the guard asked me.

"To the Munich railway station," I answered brusquely, and showed the bogus letter provided by Wolkowicz, which stated that I was a functionary on the way from Munich to Paris. The guard let me pass.

Munich was on the route of returning American soldiers. The station itself was bombed out, and the Allied command was headquartered in a huge tent.

"I'm hungry," Wolkowicz remarked, when we arrived at the Munich station. "Would you like to see the American Red Cross in action? We can get free food and coffee in their tent."

"I could stand that. Lead the way."

At the Red Cross tent, I had my first taste of American donuts, after which we found the army billets.

"You sleep here with the non-commissioned personnel," Wolkowicz directed. "I'm going to the officers' quarters. See you in the morning."

Wolkowicz gave a high sign meaning, "so far, so good," and left.

The next morning, we met again, and boarded a train. Wolkowicz put me in the third class section, and once again disappeared into the officers' quarters. Slouching all around the car were gum-chewing American soldiers, with their legs up on the benches. I quickly singled out the Jewish soldiers, and started to talk with them. With my broken English and natural proclivity for conversation, I was soon immensely enjoying this first contact with Americans. However, I kept the talk superficial, not wanting to attract too much attention since I was traveling with false papers.

The train stopped along the way for meals in restaurants. I could hardly believe this. In the Russian army, the soldiers presented their mess kits for their meager rations, but the Americans had abundant, good food on tables!

After two nights on the train, we arrived in Paris, where it was cold and rainy. I had only a thin raincoat. As I was leaving the train, I spied an abandoned army coat and took it. I did not feel too guilty about appropriating the coat. The Americans had extravagant provisions, and left boots, clothing, and other equipment lying around unattended, indicating to my mind that any loss could be easily replaced. What a contrast to the scarcity of material goods in the Russian army!

At the Gare de l'Este, Wolkowicz helped me check my baggage.

"Go to the restroom and shave," he instructed once more. "I'll be at the officers' mess, and I'll meet you later."

I never saw him again. Clean-shaven, I waited several horus for Wolkowicz, but the Captain did not appear. I checked the baggage room and saw that Wolkowicz' luggage was still there. I assumed that my companion had met some friends or a girl who had detained him. The two of us were supposed to go on to Brussels, but as the hours passed, it became clear that I had been abandoned and was on my own. At least I was thankful that Wolkowicz got me out of Germany.

Beyond that favor, I was stranded. I had no money, knew no French, and was wearing an UNRRA uniform for which I had no proper papers or identification. I knew no one in Paris. On that cold, drizzly afternoon in February, 1946, I paced back and forth in front of the Gare de l'Este, trying to decide what to do. Finally, I collected myself, thinking that, after all, I had lived through exile in Siberia; I could live through anything else.

CHAPTER 9

On to Palestine

Before long, I noticed soldiers flocking around a little window with a sign that read: "RTO-Railway Transport Office." In my broken English, I asked the soldiers what they were doing there, and was told that this was the place to ask for information and directions. After the last soldier left the RTO window, I stepped forward and addressed the clerk.

"Excuse me, sir. Could you tell me if there is a Jewish committee in Paris?"

"Which one?" the clerk asked.

I was overjoyed. The answer meant that I could find help in Paris.

"I don't care. I'm new here. I'll go wherever you suggest."

At the time, Paris had some twenty Jewish committees. I was sent to the Hebrew Immigrant Aid Society, which was affiliated with the Joint Jewish Committee in the United States. With the manager of the HIAS office, I could communicate in Yiddish and a little French. The agency offered temporary lodging and food, and gave me directions. Lugging two monstrous bags of clothing, I followed instructions and boarded the Paris subway, the Metro. Then by bus, I reached the Jewish section, called "the Place." It was a shabby area, sporting second and third class hotels, bars, and brothels. Wending my way through the streets, I finally arrived at the Herbergement on Rue des Rosiers in the fourth Arrondisement, which was a Jewish type of rescue mission. The building was filled with Jews of all ages, and their animated conversations were all about going to Palestine, the ancient land of the Hebrews, and now looked upon as the land of refuge for the Jews.

Everyone living in Paris was required to have a certificate of nationality in order to obtain a food ration card, so I sought this certificate from the Polish consulate in Paris.

"Thank you," the consul said as he took the completed form. "Come back in six weeks."

"Six weeks—that long?" I tried to conceal my apprehension over the length of time estimated to receive a reply from Poland.

"Yes, I'm sorry, but that's the way it is. We have hundreds of applications to process, and the mail is very slow. There's a world of refugees in Paris, you know. You'll just have to be patient."

I did not wait for the reply. I was still a fugitive from the Polish police, and having helped Jewish people to cross the border illegally, I did not think it was safe to wait for the Polish government's response. Someone I knew had been sentenced to four years in prison for the same offense. Pomeranz could still be serving his sentence.

During the three months in Paris waiting for passage to Palestine, a Polish Combatants' Organization sponsored a dance, which was attended by many Jewish young people. At the party, I was attracted to a petite girl with long blond hair, and danced with her all evening. Her name was Nicole, and we communicated in a mixture of Russian and Yiddish.

"Where are you from?" Nicole inquired of me.

"Skoczow, Poland."

"I see." Nicole well knew the fate of Polish Jews during the war.

"Where did you spend the war?"

"Here and there, mostly in Siberia."

"I see." Again, Nicole did not need details. In my two responses, she had already learned quite a bit about my background and recent history.

"And where are you going?"

"To Palestine," I replied brightly. "I can hardly wait to get there. Can you imagine it? A Jewish homeland—maybe even a Jewish state soon! A place where we can live in peace at last! Tell me about yourself, Nicole."

"My father and stepmother escaped early to Switzerland. My sister and I stayed behind with our real mother, and consequently, after Hitler captured Paris, we were taken first to Dranci and then to Auschwitz. My sister and mother died in Auschwitz. I obviously survived. My father is now back in the jewelry business in Paris. His stock of diamonds kept him and my stepmother comfortable in Switzerland. Would you like to come home with me after the dance and meet my family?"

"Why, yes! I'd be delighted to do that, Nicole. Thank you for inviting me. You are very kind to think of it."

I accepted Nicole's invitation enthusiastically. I missed my own family, and here was one that would understand my circumstances.

Nicole's family lived in a well-furnished, spacious apartment, and I was warmly received. The Russian father was a wealthy man from his jewelry business, and spoke Yiddish. My affinity with the family was soon recognized, and I continued to see Nicole. Her father seemed to be impressed with my deportment and background, and may have been thinking I would make a good son-in-law. One day, the jeweler made an offer.

"I could use a sharp young man like you in my business. I would be willing to teach you the jewelry trade, if you are interested."

I was surprised at the generous offer, and it was an excellent prospect for the future. However, I had other plans now.

"I am honored, sir, that you would consider me for such a position with you. You are very generous, and I appreciate all your hospitality. But, you see, I have definitely made up my mind to go to Palestine as soon as possible. Paris is just not the place for me. Thank you, thank you very much, but I'll be leaving soon."

"I understand, young man. If my business were not so prosperous here, I might be tempted to go to Palestine myself. The Jews are building a future there in our ancient homeland, and it would be exciting to be a part of it. May you find your happiness and prosperity in Palestine!"

The genuine respect Nicole's father expressed for my decision made me even more eager to go. Shortly after our conversation, Nicole was called to testify at trials in Nice against French people who collaborated with the Nazis. In her absence, I decided it was time to begin the journey to Palestine. I had grown attached to this warm-hearted family who wished to help me resettle my life, but Paris and the jewelry business did not appeal to me now. My eyes were on Palestine, and nothing could dissuade me from trying to get there.

In April, I traveled by night train from Paris to Marseilles, expecting to board a ship for Haifa. However, when the first one arrived, the ship was already overcrowded with refugees, and was not even allowed to dock. To explain the urgency of my situation, I spoke to the Israeli leaders in charge.

"I'm in desperate trouble. I left Poland under indictment, and the police might come looking for me any minute. I need to get out of the country as soon as possible!"

"Sure, we know. Everyone is desperate here. Are you different? You'll have to wait your turn."

The Israeli officials undoubtedly had heard many contingency stories, and shrugged mine off as a ploy to gain preference.

"Well, then, where do you suggest I go in the meantime?"

"You might join a group of young people who are lodged at

a fishing village about 30 miles south of Marseilles. They are a preparation group called 'hachsharah,' waiting to go to Palestine. I'd say that is the best place for you," an Israeli offered. "We will give you a train ticket to Marseilles, and a vehicle will take you to the village of La Ciotad."

I was delighted to accept the offer, and my excitement rose at the prospect of joining others like myself who were on their way to a new life in Palestine.

The preparation group was housed at Domaine del Eagle, a beautiful French castle, whose wealthy owners had disappeared during the war. The Israelis had rented the castle compound for their "hachsharah" group. It was a magnificent setting, the property extending to the edge of the cliffs overhanging the Mediterranean. A little fishing harbor nearby bore traces of German occupation. The walls of the latrines were covered with German graffiti. Inside the compound, flower and vegetable gardens were tended by members of the preparation group. At the time I arrived, the hachsharah consisted of eight men, four women, and a married couple, representing several nationalities. An Israeli man and wife served as houseparents to the prospective immigrants.

One of the women, the only one who was about my age, was an attractive, blond-haired, blue-eyed Parisienne named Giselle. Her parents were of Polish extraction, but Giselle was born in Paris. Sharing wartime experiences was the primary way of getting acquainted.

"Where were you during the Nazi occupation?" I asked Giselle.

"Hiding, like all French Jews who stayed in the country. French families took me in. It wasn't too bad."

I noticed that Giselle did not bear the trauma syndrome that I had seen so often. She was vivacious and outgoing.

"How did you happen to come here to the hachsharah?" I asked further.

"There are several Zionist organizations functioning in

Paris. I visited one of them and learned about this group. The war has been over for two years, but France is still not a happy place to live. Going to Palestine is the best alternative I know."

"I'm sure you're right," I agreed. "It's the same for me. My homeland is a dreary place, full of bad memories. I want to start over, and Palestine is our best hope."

Giselle and I worked together in the gardens, and often walked into the village to shop for the group. For a month, we shared our hopes and dreams, and grew fond of one another.

One day, a French policeman came to the lodge looking for me. The policeman was carrying a photograph of the wanted man. My application for a certificate of nationality had gone through the bureaucracy, and the Polish consulate in Paris had sent the information to Marseilles. Fortunately, I was not there when the policeman arrived, and when I returned to the hachsharah, my friends told me of the unexpected visitor.

"I was afraid this would happen," I explained to the houseparents. "I told the Israelis in Marseilles about my predicament, but they wouldn't believe me."

"What predicament?"

"I am wanted by the Polish police."

"What for?"

"For refusing to spy for them, and for smuggling Jewish people across the border."

The houseparents exchanged glances of concern over the information. The man pursed his lips decisively, and explained the more extensive ramifications.

"That makes you a real hot potato for us. We can't advertise the existence of our hachsharah groups. That's why we have to keep them small and scattered around the country. The British have spies in all the Mediterranean ports, trying to stop illegal immigration to Palestine. We don't want those blokes down on our heads. We'll have to send you out immediately, you understand?"

"That's fine with me. How do I get out?"

"We will inform the Israeli officials at the port. They'll send a jeep for you. Be ready to go early in the morning. Are you going alone?" The leader knew that Giselle might be going with me.

"I'll tell you that after the seder. Thank you for the assistance. I'm sorry to have caused you this trouble."

"No matter, we expect a lot of it in one form or another. Good luck!"

It was the first night of Passover, 1946. Filled with excitement, food, and red French wine, I proposed to Giselle.

"Will you marry me, and come with me tomorrow?"

Giselle's answer was more panicky than plausible. Perhaps she did not want to risk traveling with a fugitive.

"No, Eliezer, I can't marry you so suddenly. I couldn't marry anyone without the permission of my parents. I would have to go to Paris to see them first."

"But there isn't time! The ship leaves in the morning!"

"I'm sorry, Eliezer," Giselle declined again. "I hope you get to Palestine safely. Maybe we will meet there some day. I'll be coming over with the group whenever our departure is arranged."

I was disappointed at the abrupt termination of my first real romance, but was long accustomed to moving on when circumstances changed suddenly. Now I was more determined than ever to board the ship **Champolion**, which was anchored in the Marseilles harbor. At least it was a "legal" ship, although I had no boarding papers.

The British were intercepting illegal shiploads of Jewish refugees, and sending them to detention camps on the island of Cyprus to keep them out of the country. British intelligence units operated all over Europe to determine when refugee boats were scheduled to depart, in order to intercept their arrival in Palestine. Nevertheless, in less than three years, the B'rechah (flight) movement had emptied the DP camps, rescued all the Jews still able to leave, and sent them to Palestine.

By 1946, the atmosphere in Palestine was crackling with

tension. The embryo nation of Jews had been sweating and toiling to reclaim the promised homeland since the turn of the century. In 1897, at the First Zionist Congress in Basel, Switzerland, Theodor Herzl, spiritual father of the Jewish State, proclaimed the right of Jewish people to re-establish a national homeland. This right was recognized in the Balfour Declaration of 1917. However, the British, anxious to placate the Arab world, refused to carry out the Balfour Declaration. The mandate for Palestine decreed by the League of Nations gave international sanctions to the biblical and historic connection between Jews and Eretz-Israel (the Land of Israel).

The legitimate sanctions notwithstanding, in 1946, the British government implemented plans to crush Jewish resistance. By a concentrated "purge" of the settlements, mass arrests, disarming of the Haganah, the detention of Jewish Agency executives, and widespread military operations, Britain hoped to shake the Israelis from their national aspirations. Strict curfews were imposed, and armored cars cruised along deserted thoroughfares. Riots and bombings were everyday occurrences. Hundreds of young men were arrested and taken to concentration camps by the British.

When I arrived at the port in Marseilles, a young Israeli told me how to get aboard the ship.

"Grab a suitcase and make like a porter. Go up the ramp and get lost in the crowd."

The simple scheme worked, and I managed to get on board, portering my own luggage on my back.

The former troop transport converted to a passenger ship carried 1000 youth-aliyah who had certificates of immigration to Palestine, 2000 French soldiers, and about 25 Jewish stowaways. The Jewish agency supplied food for all of the Jewish passengers.

One week later, the ship reached Haifa. Lacking proper clearance, the stowaway passengers were taken under guard by

British police, and put on a separate bus. It was a minor intimidation. All of the ship's passengers were taken to the same place, a quarantine camp a few miles north of Haifa. The place resembled a prison camp familiar to many of them, but these young Jews who had survived concentration camps and other horrors were happy just to be in Palestine. The week of confinement was a joyful time. The new immigrants danced the hora, had their first taste of Israeli food, and enjoyed the warm summer weather. Everybody in the camp was looking for someone they knew—family, friends, former townsfolk—anyone who could restore some continuity with the recent past.

Consistent with the pattern of my life, it was not long before I saw a familiar face.

"Bunio Wien! Remember me?" I called out to the young man who was one of the auxillary guardians of the camp.

"Of course I do!" the red-haired youth shouted in glee. "What a surprise to see you here! Wonderful!"

Bunio Wien was one of my classmates at the teachers' institute in Stanislav. He had already been in Palestine for more than two years, and was now working as a temporary guard at the quarantine camp. Meeting Wien was a piece of providence that led to my first shelter in Palestine.

A shipmate on the **Champolion** had relatives in Haifa, but he had not been able to notify them of his coming to Palestine, nor did he know where they lived. The young man offered me shelter with his relatives when he found them. It was no trouble at all for Bunio Wien to locate the family's residence, and deliver a message to them. The family sent back a reply which assured the two of us a welcome place to stay.

For the first three weeks in the country, I lived with these people, and found a job blacktopping Haifa streets and boulevards. The job proved to be too strenuous, so I gave it up and moved to Tel Aviv. Another relative of the same shipmate offered me a job in a soap factory, but the pay was so low, I kept on the lookout for a better job. I was twenty-four years old, tired of being a fugitive and a wanderer, and now longed for a wife, home, and family.

A new appreciation for my own family heritage came by way of meeting someone from my hometown, Mr. Berman, the owner of the flour mill where I worked in Skoczow. Mr. Berman had lost three things since I had last seen him, his goiter, his paunch, and the flour mill. He appeared at my door one day.

"Mr. Berman! Come in! How in the world did you find me?"

"You aren't familiar yet with our most effective grapevine?" Berman laughed. "It's pretty easy to find someone in our small country. Everyone knows someone who knows someone, etc. I'm glad to see you here. Much has happened since we last saw one another, nu? I escaped from Poland with my family early in the war, and we came to Palestine several years ago. We feel like natives now. How about you? Where have you been all this time?"

Mr. Berman listened intently while I told him about my own odyssey as a displaced person. The elder man's face registered deep compassion for the son of his old friend, Heiman Urbach. I was touched by my former employer's expression of feeling for my family.

"Your father would be proud of you, Eliezer. I'm so sorry to hear about your brother and your parents. I owed your father a great deal of gratitude, and so did many other people in Skoczow. During the first World War, Heiman helped me financially, and gave me good business advice. He also provided bread for hungry people during the war. He was a good and generous man."

"Thank you for telling me that, Mr. Berman. I'm glad to know these things. My respect for my father continues to grow with every story I hear about him. I hope I will never dishonor his name."

I lived in a boarding house during the first summer after arriving in Palestine. I became friendly with another resident, a German Jewish boy named Joseph, who had survived the war in

Switzerland. Joseph was traditionally religious, and prayed with phylacteries. On Rosh Hashanah, Joseph prepared to go to the New Year Service at the Great Synagogue in Tel Aviv.

"Eliezer, come with me to the service," Joseph urged. "We must say kaddish for our parents."

Nostalgia and grief welled up in my heart, and I agreed to go with Joseph.

"You are right, Joseph. My memories are painful, too. I haven't been to a synagogue for a long time. Maybe it will help."

A doorkeeper met us at the entrance of the Synagogue.

"Where are your tickets?" the bearded man asked.

Joseph told him, "We are refugees from Europe, and arrived just a short time ago. Could we just have a standing place? We want to say kaddish for our parents who died in concentration camps."

"I'm sorry, gentlemen," the doorkeeper replied sternly. "No tickets, no entrance."

This incident marked one of the saddest days of my life. I had clung, albeit weakly, to the religion of my people. Papa's blessing had been significant and precious to me, and I recalled it many, many times during my struggle to survive the camps and homelessness. It seemed to me that every Jew had a religious heritage. After all, God himself called the Jews into existence as a special people. To ignore God's existence diluted Jewish identity. At least that was my own experience. As I stared past the doorkeeper into the crowded synagogue, shock turned to bitterness. Our exclusion from the service was beyond my comprehension, and strained the ties to Judaism to the breaking point. It was the last time I tried to worship in a synagogue. The religious aspect of my Jewishness died, to be resurrected another day in another place.

ॐ

A new job opened up in the summer of 1946 in Ramat Gan, outside of Tel Aviv. My Uncle Isadore from Brazil, had written a friend, a textile factory owner, to hire his nephew. I was happy in Ramat Gan, saved some money, and bought some clothes. At the corner grocery where I shopped, I made friends with the grocer and his family, who were Polish Jews. The Trutiak family were very compatible, and invited me to their home for supper occasionally. Finding people with whom I had a great deal in common made me feel more at ease and accepted in the new country. To my surprise, one evening Mrs. Trutiak posed a question.

"Would you like to meet a young lady?"

Eliezer, on arrival in Paris wearing UNRRA uniform

Eliezer, age 26, after landing in Palestine

CHAPTER 10

A New Life and Another War

Nahum Leiner had been a Zionist most of his life, active in the Jewish movement, and constantly helped Jewish people in a variety of ways. His son and daughter attended Hebrew schools in Poland, their original home. He was not a wealthy man, but the values stressed in his home were friendship, love, ambition, and education.

I met Sara, Nahum's daughter, during Chanukah. Mrs. Trutiak took me to the Leiners' apartment and introduced me to Mrs. Leiner, Samuel, and Sara. Mr. Leiner was sick in the hospital at the time. Together we celebrated the Feast of Dedication with potato pancakes, sour cream, and tea, and I was treated as an honored guest. That evening, Sara and I went for a walk to get acquainted. Sara was shy, and waited for me to initiate the conversation.

"Your mother is a very witty lady," I commented. "I enjoyed visiting with her. Your brother is an interesting fellow, too. I'm sorry your father is ill. Will he be home from the hospital soon?"

The ease with which I made conversation in my halting Hebrew seemed to impress Sara, although I often had to switch to Polish to finish a sentence.

"Your Hebrew is not too bad for having been in the country less than a year. My father would like that. I'm glad you like my family. You should meet Abba, you will like him, too. He is seriously ill with tuberculosis, but we hope he will be able to come home again. I'm wondering where you appeared from—out of the cold?"

"Siberia **was** cold," I laughed. "The climate is much hotter here, and I don't mean just the weather! The political air is too hot for my liking."

"When you live in a Zionist family, you get used to that kind of heat," Sara remarked bluntly. "We're in for a war, that's for sure, but Ben-Gurion has the situation well-organized. When the British leave, we will have a Jewish state."

"Do you think so, Sara? I hope you are right. That's why I came to Palestine—to find a happy place to live. How long have you been here?"

"Abba came in 1936 and sent for the rest of us about a year later. He was a Zionist even in Poland. As an accountant, he worked with German businessmen. When Hitler came to power, they warned Abba that the Jews were being mistreated in Germany, and advised him to go to Palestine before worse things began to happen. My father took the good advice."

"You were very fortunate to have gotten out so early, and here you've been for ten years already!"

After an hour or so, we returned to the apartment, and I thanked the Leiners for their hospitality. Turning to Sara, I asked if I could come to see her again.

"Yes, of course. You are welcome here any time. But next time, no Polish—only Hebrew. If you're going to be an Israeli, you must stick to your new language! Shalom, Eliezer."

The next day, when I returned to visit Sara, Samuel drew me aside before she appeared.

"Are your intentions toward my sister serious?" Samuel inquired with prudent brotherly concern.

"Yes," I replied without hesitation. "She is a nice girl, and I believe she will make me happy. I hope I can make her happy, too. But, Samuel, I am in no financial position to get married right away."

"Don't worry about that. We'll help you with the finances. Go ahead and make your wedding plans."

Six weeks later, Sara and I were married, on January 28, 1947. It was not otherwise a peaceful day. A curfew was in effect, and throughout the city, riots and bombings erupted sporadically. Two British tanks were stationed nose to nose on the main road to Tel Aviv. Palestine was in birth pangs. The State of Israel was about to be born. After 2000 years of exile, the Jews were going to see a promise fulfilled.

After our wedding, Sara and I moved into a settlement for new immigrants outside of Tel Aviv. The settlement, called Givat Shmuel, "the Hill of Samuel," consisted of two large buildings which housed sixteen families each. The living quarters were small, but there were conveniences such as running water, and there was a clinic for mothers and children. The first year in the settlement was an exciting and happy time for us.

On November 29, 1947, the United Nations passed a resolution on the partition of Palestine, calling for the establishment of the Jewish state. All Tel Aviv danced in the streets. Old men, young men, women, girls, and children shouted and sang, "A Jewish Land." Even some of the British soldiers joined in the celebration.

The celebration was short-lived. From surrounding countries, Arab soldiers stirred up the Arab villages and blockaded Jerusalem, attempting to thwart the U.N. resolution with terrorism. Bombs exploded under railway bridges, grenades were thrown at buses while passing through Arab towns. All Palestine could feel the preparation for a bitter eye-for-eye and tooth-for-tooth war. The Arabs attacked the settlements, burned homes, and disrupted communication lines.

Every man in the settlements who was able, was called to guard duty. The men bought their own shotguns and patrolled the settlement borders. Only two villages separated Givat Shmuel from the Arab border. People were killed on guard duty. A Romanian Jew, with whom I worked at the factory, was cut to pieces by the Arabs.

In Givat Shmuel, one of the members of the Haganah, the underground guerrilla army, approached me one morning.

"Come and join the forces, Urbach. We need volunteers, especially men who have had military experience."

"I've had enough of war," I told the recruiter. "I'm tired of the shooting, fighting, and killing. If you have the authority to draft me, of course, I would come. But I won't join voluntarily right now. My time to fight is coming soon enough!"

The Jews were desperately short of weapons. Preparing for withdrawal, the British gave their weapons to the Arabs. On May 14, 1948, the last of the British staff left Palestine, and the Mandate era ended. In a short ceremony at a gathering of all Jewish leaders in Tel Aviv, David Ben-Gurion read the Proclamation of Independence of the State of Israel. Within eight hours after the public announcement came over the radio that Israel was an independent State, the Arab armies began to invade Israel. Egyptian planes bombed the Tel Aviv area.

On May 15, every able-bodied Israeli was drafted into the army. I packed my Russian army shirt to take with me. It was the custom of the Russians to carry a clean shirt to be used as a shroud if killed in battle. My time of peace had been of very short duration.

"I don't know if I will ever see you again, Sara. Chances aren't too good. Take the baby and go to your mother's place while I'm gone. It will be better than staying alone."

"I'd rather stay here," Sara insisted bravely, "but I'll see how it works out. Don't worry, I'll do what I think is best for us. We'll be all right, and so will you, Eliezer."

There was little else Sara could say. Neither she nor any other Jewish wife, mother, or sweetheart had a choice. The prospect of an Arab victory was frightening to contemplate.

Everyone knew the odds. A nation of 650,000 Jews was contending in battle with nations totaling over 40 million. The Arab armies drew forces from Egypt, Jordan, Syria, Iraq, and Saudi Arabia.

"I wish I could be optimistic, too, Sara. Somehow, I have a firm conviction that God will not let Israel perish, but I don't have much hope for my own survival under the circumstances. I'll be back if I haven't used up all my mazal."

It was extremely difficult for me to leave the new family life I had so recently established. Less than a month after the partition of Palestine was declared in 1947, a daughter was born to us. We named her Nechama, a Hebrew word meaning "joy" or "comfort," after her maternal grandfather Nahum, who had died a few months earlier.

Following my induction into the Israel Defense Forces, I was taken to a former British camp site. I was grouped with men who had previous military experience, mostly Jewish deserters from the Polish and Russian armies. Many of them had military rank. At the camp especially designed for artillery, we were given a week of instruction in gunnery. The weapons were field guns and munitions from France, including a 1901 model of a 65-millimeter French mountain gun, called Canon de Montaigne. The guns were made so that they could be dismantled and moved from place to place, a useful feature in view of the weapon shortage. After a short explanation of how to use the guns, the men were sent to defend settlements in need of artillery support.

Our first mission was an infantry night raid on an Arab outpost at Negba, in the northern Negev. Located at a crossroads, the station was strategically important, since it blocked off communications and supplies to a newly-formed chain of agricultural settlements in the Negev. From the Negba station, the Arabs shelled and destroyed the nearby kibbutz. The outpost was a former British police station, one in a chain of fortified square buildings which were built to hold siege for weeks. Called

Tiegart buildings, they were supplied with food, had storage for munitions, and radio communications. The British left most of these fortresses to the Arabs.

Shelling from a position in an orange grove, our unit barely scratched the surface of the iron and concrete building. Our military equipment was insufficient, and the soldiers were inexperienced at firing the old mountain guns. The unsuccessful raid was disheartening to the poorly-equipped and out-numbered Israeli soldiers. Morale was dealt another blow when the Egyptians blocked off all roads leading to the Negev, and furloughs home became impossible. During this long separation, I became despondent with concern for my family.

As a corporal, I had a number of men under my orders. When we were not engaged in fighting, we patrolled or moved to more strategic positions. In the summer of 1948, after shelling an Arab village, we were all invited for supper in a nearby kibbutz. I was surprised to see a girl named Hannah at one of the tables. Hannah was a member of the preparation group in Marseilles.

"Hannah! You're the first one I've seen from the hachsharah! So you are a kibbutznik now! It's so good to see you."

"Yes, and Giselle is here, too," Hannah said quietly.

"Really? Tell her I'm here, would you? I'd like to see her, too."

"I'll go and fetch her right now."

Giselle appeared shortly, and sat down to talk with me. Neither of us was very comfortable with the meeting, and conversation was strained.

"How long have you been here, Giselle?" I began stiffly. "You look well. How are you getting along?"

"A little over a year. I'm doing all right. I was going to get in touch with you, but I heard right away that you were married, so I didn't bother you."

"Yes, that's right. I found a nice girl for a wife, and I have a little daughter already."

"That's nice."

"And you? Are you married?"

"No, I'm still single. Too bad you came over to fight another war, but I guess we all knew it could happen. I must say, hachsharah was more exciting than feeding chickens on this kibbutz."

I intended to keep the conversaion impersonal, and steered away from any allusion to our previous relationship. I still resented the way it had ended, and I had no regrets now.

"In Marseilles, it was easy to overlook the mundane work necessary to make the Zionist dream come true. We couldn't be so much prepared for that reality. Feeding chickens and milking cows seems a long way from 'building a Jewish state,' but the dreamers have to eat, you know. As far as the war is concerned, it's too bad we have to fight for our existence, but, on the other hand, fighting is better than being put up the chimney like we were in Europe. No one will accuse us of being led to slaughter like dumb sheep again."

"Of course, you're right, Eliezer. I didn't mean to sound complaining. You have the hard job. Good luck in soldiering. I really have to be going now. It was good to see you again. Shalom."

Whatever second thoughts Giselle may have had about rejecting my proposal of marriage, she could see that I had found a new life in Palestine, and she was happy for me. She left the dining hall quickly and did not look back.

After the lonely duty in the Negev, I was sent to another camp. With additional training, I received a crew of new immigrants who had recently been released from detention camps on Cyprus, and some others to train, and we all became part of the Second Artillery Regiment. The Regiment was dispatched to the Judean hills to establish communication lines to Jerusalem, which was freed in 1948 after a year-long siege. The people in Jerusalem had suffered from hunger and thirst, even though a "Burma road" was built in the early summer of 1948.

The Regiment's mission was to strengthen the Israeli positions, and to enlarge the narrow pass of land tying Jerusalem to the main territory.

My unit had an unfortunate experience at Tzorah, the biblical birthplace of Samson. We were positioned on a hill to bombard Beth Gemal, a Catholic monastery which was occupied by the Egyptians. Located on the road from the Negev to Jerusalem, the Egyptians were harassing Israeli traffic from their position in the monastery. The Israeli infantry was preparing for an all-out attack, following the artillery barrage.

"Men, our objective is to soften up the Egyptians, and drive them out of the monastery. The Palmach is waiting for our support," the officer-in-charge directed. "Fire your salvos on command!"

Three guns in the battery sent their shells whizzing toward the target. The officer-in-charge commanded my unit to fire its fifty shells. But when I gave the order for the gunner to pull the trigger, the gun recoiled and no shell came out. The munitions were old and would not fire. Frantically, the gunners removed the dead shell from the barrel, but they could not find the two handles to wind the gun's spring back into position to fire again.

"Where are the handles? Without the handles we can't shoot!" I screamed at the men. "Find them!"

With much cursing and mutual blaming, the gunners searched wildly for the handles, under tarpaulins, tents, and munition boxes. Meanwhile, the officer was shouting,

"Gun number four, fire!"

To no avail. Gun number four was defunct. Nevertheless, the other guns in the battery continued to fire, and the Israelis soon took the monastery. After the Egyptians were cleared out, the soldiers camped in the monastery, where we met the padres, nuns, missionaries, and Armenian workers. The Italian monks, who operated an agricultural school for Arabs there, were hospitable and shared everything but their faith with the soldiers. Some of our battle troops, previously Haganah guerrillas, machine-gunned the wine kegs in the cellar and caught the red liquid in their messkits. Hundreds of gallons of wine poured out onto the floor.

The battery stayed six weeks in the thick-walled, spacious monastery. Oddly, I made no connection between the Polish Catholicism so prominent in my native country, and the monks here. The monastery seemed strangely out of context, a foreign body on the landscape. I wandered into the church a few times, but only out of curiosity. Jewish soldiers billeted in a Catholic monastery that ministered to Arab farmers was a bizarre set of circumstances that was not conducive to religious sentiment.

The padres spoke English, and since I was one of the few Israelis who could speak this language reasonably well, I had more conversation with them. The non-Jewish population was under curfew and could not move around freely. Consequently, when the monastery residents needed medicine, the padres asked me to journey to Jerusalem and Tel Aviv to replenish the medicinal supplies. They expressed their gratitude by inviting me to have lunch with them, and gave me some wine to take home on my next furlough.

The Second Artillery Regiment occupied posts in Jerusalem during the winter of 1948-49. Because there was so much leisure time, the soldiers became restless. The commander of the battery summoned me to his quarters.

"Urbach, tomorrow you are going to be sent to a school in downtown Jerusalem to take a course in singing."

"Singing? Yes, sir. May I ask for what purpose, sir?"

"It's a course in folklore and Israeli folk songs, actually. We need to raise morale around here and keep the soldiers out of mischief. When you get back, you are assigned to teach what you have learned to the rest of us. Singing together is better than boring card games all day long."

I learned more than twenty Israeli folk songs for this assignment, and the commander was right.

At last, the war came to an end, and the armistice treaty was signed in June, 1949. The Israelis had driven the Arabs out of Galilee and the Negev.

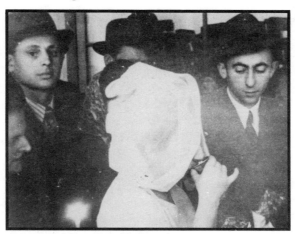

Wedding of Eliezer and Sara

Eliezer in the Israeli army, Independence War

CHAPTER 11

Immigration to Brazil

During my long absence, Sara took the baby and moved in with her mother when she could no longer pay the rent at Givat Shmuel. Army pay was inadequate for her living expenses. Awaiting me when I arrived home was a bill for nine months of unpaid rent.

With hope for better days, we moved back to Givat Shmuel and found the apartment dirty. Field mice had eaten holes in the blankets, and spiders shuttled across the floor.

"Oh, but it's good to be back home!" I sighed with relief and contentment. "I couldn't be happier if I were a king and this were a palace!"

"A palace it's not," Sara rejoined, picking up a rug and making a cloud of dust with it. "In any case, the royal varmints will have to go!"

"Yes, of course, Sara. We'll have it cleaned up in no time. Let's just be thankful that we are alive and able to come back here."

"That's true, Eliezer. Things could be worse. We are all well, and you have your old job back at the textile factory. Compared to the new immigrants, we are well off."

"The job is no big bonanza, Sara. The pay scale is low, and

it's piece work. We won't be able to save any money, but at least we can eat and pay the rent on my salary."

These were times of hardship and privation. Israel was in serious economic trouble, yet the new State opened its doors to all Jewish people. Many thought of Israel as a home and a haven even though life there was very difficult. Meat and clothing were rationed, and jobs were scarce.

In 1951, I was laid off my job. After several weeks without work, I encountered a Polish Jew named Joe. We had met before the war, shortly after my arrival in Palestine. A small man with a homely face, a bald head, and a warm heart, Joe was a civilian clerk and accountant at army headquarters.

"How are you doing, Eliezer?" Joe asked cheerfully.

"I have to tell you, I've been better."

"Why so glum? Can I be of any help?"

"I don't know if you can, Joe. I've been out of work for several weeks, and I have a wife and family to support somehow."

"So that's the problem, eh? Well, maybe I can help." Joe slapped me on the arm encouragingly. "You've been a good army man, haven't you? I'd say we need your experience at headquarters. I'll see if I can get you a job of some kind with the military, all right?"

"That would be very good of you. I hadn't really considered working for the army again, but you're right—I have some experience there. I'll wait to hear from you, and thanks much, Joe."

Soon after his promise to investigate a job possibility, Joe invited me to army headquarters.

"Captain Prizan, sir, this is the man I told you about, Eliezer Urbach, former corporal in the IDF."

"Good of you to come, Urbach. Do you understand munitions?"

"Yes, sir. I handled munitions during the Independence War. I was in an artillery regiment."

"Fine. We need someone who knows how to classify, store, and use munitions. I can see that you are qualified. You can go to work immediately as a civilian clerk in this department."

Having spent so much time in the Russian and Israeli armies, I felt at home in the army camp. I wore no uniform, but enjoyed all the privileges of non-com and commissioned officers. However, there were some drawbacks. The wages were still low, and the army camp was a two-hour walk, or one hour by bicycle, from the settlement. I worked six days a week, long hours, and had to carry most of the food for the family home on my back. In February, 1951, we had a new baby, a little boy whom we named Chaim, after his paternal grandfather. By summer, I was discouraged and exhausted from trying to support my family on a job so far from home for so little pay. I had to think of something else to do.

"Sara, we are going to move to Tishbi along with some other ex-soldiers and their families," I announced one day.

"Tishbi? What is that?"

"A new settlement of Karen Kayemet land. The government is leasing 500 dunams to a group of us. We each get 20 dunams to farm."

Sara was not endowed with an adventuresome spirit, and having two babies to care for, practical questions arose quickly in her mind.

"How far is it?"

"South, near Rishon le Zion."

"Is there anything there? A store? Electricity? Water?"

"No, no, no, nothing yet."

"Is there even a road to the settlement?"

"No."

"Oi Vey! You are taking me to a desert!"

"We won't be alone, Sara," I consoled. "Four other families will be there. You know how I like to work on the land. It's a 99-year lease, but the lessee has to be on the land or the government will give it to someone else. It will be all right!"

Sara was not convinced that giving up our little apartment in Givat Shmuel and moving with the children to an even more tenuous situation was a good idea, but I had hopes for the experiment.

The new settlement was located ten miles south of Tel Aviv. In a large Arab house surrounded by a high wall, each settler family lived in one of the five rooms. The conditions were primitive, the sanitation poor, and we had to carry water a long distance from a well. The artesian well was not functioning properly, which caused many problems with the water supply. Snakes and scorpions were commonplace. It was not exactly Gan Eden.

Although I had hoped to be a farmer, the settlement clearly was not the answer to the family's existence. The land would not be divided among the settlers for many months, my work demanded long hours, and I did not have the stamina to stay on and wait for the land arrangement to be completed. We began to think about leaving Israel.

A year before we joined the new settlement, my Uncle Isadore Fabiskiewicz, an importer and exporter of office equipment in Brazil, had written and asked us to come to Brazil. Uncle Henry and his wife, Luba, had also immigrated to Brazil from Munich, and Henry now worked as a design painter of rugs in a textile factory. Isadore, like Henry, was in debt to his sister, Berta, and Heiman Urbach for help in hard times. In the late 1930's, my parents helped Isadore to go to college in Vienna, since being a Jew prevented him from going to school in Poland. Heiman loaned Isadore five thousand dollars in American money, which at that time, could not be brought legally across the border into Poland. The American money came from Berta's brother-in-law in Czechoslovakia. The transaction involved grave risk. Fourteen years old at the time, I accompanied my mother when she went to pick up the money. We traveled by horse-drawn sled through the snow to Czechoslovakia. Isadore waited at the border on the

Polish side. With the money hidden on her person, I watched the border guards search my pale and frightened mother, but they did not find the money.

Considering the family debt, I began to think that my two uncles in Brazil might provide the means for a better life for me and my family in that country. During the Fall and Winter of 1953, I applied for visas several times at the Brazilian consulate in Tel Aviv.

Many people became dissatisfied with Israel at the same time, and left the country. Extensive rationing had created a great black market in commodities. Goods and money were unfairly distributed, and while the profiteers grew more prosperous, the poor people became poorer.

The visas were finally granted. However, in the meantime, another letter had come from Uncle Isadore asking us **not** to come to Brazil. Isadore explained that his financial situation was strained, and he was afraid the Urbach family would be an additional burden. His wife, Erna, had recently brought her sister over from Europe, and did not want the responsibility of another family on her hands. But it was too late to change my mind. I was determined to go, whether or not the relatives received us.

While I waited for the visas to be processed at the Brazilian consulate, a Brazilian Jew who had immigrated to Israel and now wanted to return to Brazil, remarked to me, "If there were a bridge across the ocean, you could see Jews crossing it both ways with their bags on their backs."

"Why is that?" I asked, more to be conversational than to be informed. I already knew the answer. My own bags were on my back, as I mentally prepared to emigrate to another country.

"You know why," the fellow went on, shaking his head sadly. "Jews everywhere are dissatisfied and looking for a peaceful life. After our experience in Hitler's Europe, and disappointment with the hard life in Israel, plus continual conflict and war with the Arabs, many are on the move again. Brazil is a popular place because it is open to immigration, and doesn't have restrictive government policies, like the United States and other countries. But many don't find what they are looking for there either. The Jews are still wandering. I guess I'm one of the lucky ones. At least I can 'wander' back to where I came from. European Jews don't all have that option, especially Polish Jews."

As he finished, the man was staring wistfully out of the window, and became lost in his own thoughts. The Brazilian was right, painfully so, I thought to myself. But I preferred to keep hope alive, and believe that we would see better days in Brazil.

"Here are your visas, sir," the consulate official at the desk said at last. "The documents are all in order. I hope you like our country."

"Thank you very much. I hope so, too. Good afternoon, sir."

The visas seemed to be an answer to the intolerable situation at home. Eight months after the harsh settlement experiment, we moved back into the apartment of Sara's mother in Ramat Gan. Five people were crowded into two small rooms. Although Mrs. Leiner was a kind and generous woman who had room in her heart for her beloved family, the living space was another matter. Sara's father had left some money and property to his children when he died. With Samuel's legal assistance, Sara's inheritance was obtained, and the money was just enough to buy boat tickets to Brazil for the family.

Early in 1954, we packed our belongings, and sold our furniture to Sara's mother. Mrs. Leiner cried at the railroad station as her family left for the port of Haifa. Her grandchildren were her pride and joy. Nechama was six, and Chaim was almost three years old. It seemed as if we were always saying goodbye.

"You are always taking my grandchildren from me!" Mrs. Leiner protested bitterly. "Why do you have to go to Brazil?"

"You have to understand, Savta," I reasoned in vain with my mother-in-law. "I can't provide for my family in Israel. We are tired of the struggle here. There is no peace. Hopefully, life will be better for us in Brazil. My uncles have done well there, and maybe I will, too. We will write to you often, and send pictures of the children. Thank you for all your help and generosity. We love you very much and want you to take good care of yourself while we're gone."

As we left the tearful grandmother and boarded the train, I had no idea how applicable the Brazilian Jew's statement would be to my own family. We would be on the bridge back to Israel sooner than I thought.

✌️

It was a rough crossing from Haifa to Marseilles. The women and children aboard the ship became seasick and vomited frequently. I was not afflicted with seasickness, and enjoyed the trip immensely, reading, resting, and taking care of the children when needed. A week later, we landed at Marseilles.

A Jewish man with the shipping agency placed us at a hotel, where we stayed for three days. Chaim became fascinated with the hotel chamber pot, which was porcelain and brightly painted. In a typical three-year-old manner, he insisted upon taking the pot with us on the ship. The good-natured hotel manager wanted to accommodate our little boy's request, but I declined the offer. The family was already loaded with paraphenalia, which I had to lug on my back.

At Marseilles, we boarded a French ship called **Provence**. Many of the other passengers were Italian and Spanish people who were also leaving their respective countries because of economic problems, and immigrating to Argentina or Brazil. We traveled third class, deep in the ship at the level of the waves, and were quartered dormitory style, the men separated from the women and children. Our traveling companions were simple peasant folk. As usual, I had a grand time making new friends. At the equator, the passengers celebrated the traditional way with cheap French wine, but I could not join the Mardi Gras spirit of the occasion. The responsibilities I had assumed as a family man, and the uncertainty of the immediate future kept a festive mood in abeyance.

The ship **Provence** docked at Rio de Janiero for a few hours. A stifling heat wave hit us as we disembarked for a view of the city. Brazil was in the middle of a tropical summer. The steaming hot sun soon had us drenched in perspiration, and a tour of the city was a soggy experience.

From Rio de Janiero, I sent Uncle Isadore a telegram telling him when we would be arriving at Santos. The telegram was written in Portuguese, which I had begun to learn from a Brazilian Jewish boy on the ship. He gave me a Portuguese self-teaching booklet in exchange for a few instructions in Polish/Hebrew-stricken English. The Jewish boy was "crossing the bridge" again; having immigrated to Israel, he became discouraged with kibbutz life, and was returning to Brazil.

On February 26, 1954, we arrived in the port of Santos on the way to Sao Paulo. Uncle Isadore, his wife, Erna, and Luba were waiting at the dock to take us to Sao Paulo.

"So you have arrived!" Isadore greeted us.

"Yes! For much luck, and peace!" I replied exuberantly.

"You try here. You will see," Isadore checked my optimism. "Things aren't so rosy here either. Remember, I didn't advise you to come. But it's good to see you and the children anyway!"

"Where are we going to stay?" I asked, as we loaded up Isadore's Plymouth.

"With Henry and me for the time being," Luba answered. "We don't have much space, but we'll manage until you find work and get a place of your own."

"That's very kind of you, Luba. We're grateful for that. I'll look for work right away. Surely it won't take long. Meanwhile, we'll start learning Portuguese while we're settling into the country."

It was a two-hour drive along a winding road to Sao Paulo, which was located high on a plateau in the mountains. The oppressive heat, tropical scenery, exotic animal and bird life presented an overwhelming contrast to anything we had experienced before.

"It certainly is a strange, new land, something like entering Israel the first time. We'll have to make adjustments to this change of climate and way of life, but I'm sure we will manage to do so shortly." My gurgling, school-boy enthusiasm seemed to be irritating Isadore.

"It may be more difficult than you imagine. But now you are here, and Henry and I will help you get settled. I will inquire around about a job for you."

Uncle Henry lived in a small, one-bedroom apartment, but graciously took the four of us in for six weeks. Isadore visited often, and helped pay for our upkeep.

Henry gave us a warning early after our arrival.

"Don't you dare tell anyone that you are Jewish, or that you have come from Israel."

"Why not? Why should we hide our identity? Is there persecution here?"

"No, but there are many Nazis here, and you never know who might hit you," Henry explained. "Just be careful, and do as I say."

In accordance with Henry's advice, Sara and I counseled with the children.

"Nobody speaks Hebrew outside the house," I ordered. "We don't want to cause any unnecessary problems. We will tell the neighbors we came from Germany, and we will learn to speak Portuguese as quickly as possible."

When I applied for a Brazilian identity card, the red stamp on my visa, designating my working classification, was transferred to the card. All immigrants to Brazil were required to declare their professional status. I had certified myself as a citrus grower, based upon my experience at the settlement outside of Tel Aviv. A fact unknown to me at the time was that agricultural workers were not allowed to live in the city, and because Uncle Isadore had refused to send a letter of sponsorship, the red stamp prevented me from living or working in the city. After coming all this way in search of a more prosperous existence in Brazil, I was destined to be a low-paid agricultural worker.

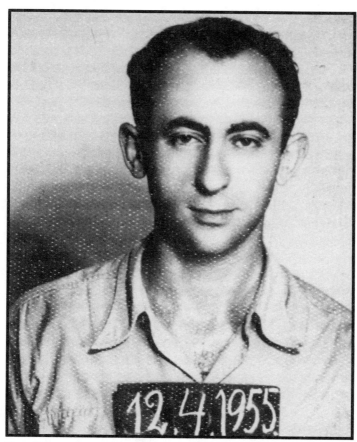

Brazilian passport photo

Left to right standing, Vasco, Sara,
Henry and wife, Luba Bottom, Chaim,
Eliezer, and Nechama

Laerte Modolo and family

CHAPTER 12

Hard Times in Brazil

Rio Bonito, "Beautiful River," was the name of the little village where I took my family to live, and try to eke out a living. Uncle Isadore found a job for me as caretaker of a rich man's summer estate, twenty-five miles outside of Sao Paulo. I hired a station wagon to haul our few belongings to the location. My work was to take care of the two houses, garage and grounds, a vegetable garden, and the flower beds. The employer paid me 2000 cruzeros a month, about sixty-five dollars, and I was expected to become self-supporting eventually, from the sale of farm produce.

Most of the neighbors in the village were also caretakers, laborers, or farm hands. Meat and cheese were available in a covered market place, and a neighbor's son brought milk. River and lake fish could be bought from a resident fisherman.

Cows resembling the scrawny cows of Egypt grazed in a pasture close to a nearby ravine. The animals were a striking contrast to the fat cows in Israel. The Brazilian cows were also covered with welts caused by flies that implanted their eggs under the skin. The welts then filled with maggots. The bleeding welts were a gruesome sight.

The climate was tropical, very humid and uncomfortable.

Inland, where we were located, it was steamy hot in summer without the benefit of cooling sea breezes. The first task I undertook was to build a large chicken pen, and then I started to work the extensive assignment of land. Many problems hindered progress. The water pump frequently failed to function, and I did not understand the ways and seasons of Brazilian agriculture. Weeds and undergrowth overran my ability to cover the territory alone. After three frustrating months, the impatient landowner asked me to leave.

"I'm sorry I couldn't get things going sooner," I apologized. "There are many ways of doing things here that I am not used to yet."

"My land won't wait until you learn," the owner grumbled, "and I thought I was hiring a family of laborers. One man can't do it by himself. Return the key to the house, and I will pay your back wages."

I was crushed at the harsh dismissal. I had never been fired from a job before, and I had worked hard at the assignment. I never intended to make laborers of Sara and the children, and was unaware that the landowner had expected this. It was an unfortunate beginning for us as new immigrants.

We collected our belongings once again to move on, but when I returned the house key, the German landlord refused to pay the 1000 cruzeros owed to me in back wages, claiming that I had not earned the money. Now I was penniless and unemployed. It was humiliating to go back to my uncles for help, but there was no other recourse.

Henry found another job for me in a textile factory, utilizing my five years of experience as a weaver in Israel. Henry also provided some money to get the family settled in Americana where the factory was located, fifty kilometers from Sao Paulo. I left Sara and the children at Rio Bonito while I went to try the new work at the factory. I stayed at a boarding house which served rice and red beans twice a day, and very little meat. The food was greasy and unappetizing.

The factory was a rayon textile plant named Citra, which employed 1500 workers. Several spinneries and large eucalyptus plantations were in the vicinity. The factory made rayon from eucalyptus pulp. The pulp was treated with sulfuric acid, blown through sieves, and spun. The fibers were weak, consequently, the material was fragile. The factory also produced taffeta, organdy, and some artificial silk materials from which shirts for men, dresses and blouses for women were made. Since the clothing was of poor quality and wore out quickly in the hot, humid climate, there was a great demand for the products.

The factory operated at full steam, sometimes two shifts. I worked from 6:00 a.m. until 5:00 p.m., with a half-hour lunch break. I served two wide looms, and later, another small loom. The fragile fibers broke often and slowed production. Tending two or three looms, difficult as it was, brought no more money than I earned as a caretaker. The work was piece work, and pay was according to how much a worker produced. The rickety machines also broke down frequently, curtailing output.

There was little ventilation in the factory, and it was oppressively hot, July, 1954. To my dismay, the conditions were considerably worse and more primitive than in Israel. The decision to come to Brazil seemed to be another fiasco destined to end with the dissolution of my hopes for a normal, happy, and productive life.

Having a family to support, and no other job in sight, I was in bondage to the situation. After working two weeks, I brought Sara and the children to Americana. The town had been founded and named by Southern refugees from the Civil War in the United States. Some Italians, whom I met at the factory, offered to rent us a tiny room with a kitchenette in their house, and we borrowed a mattress and bed. The conditions were terrible. There was no running water, and no electricity. A well and an outhouse were the only "conveniences." Charcoal for cooking was stored in the outhouse, hardly a sanitary arrangement, since the outhouse was merely a hole in the ground with a little shed around it.

Besides the four Urbachs, two other families and a single man lived under the same roof. The single man, Vincente, was the owner. He was a tall, slim, strong, and good-looking fellow, and always ready to lend a helping hand. In the second room were his brother, Nicola, and his wife, Ida. Nicknamed Iducca, Ida had blond hair and fair skin. Vincente's sister, Maria, and her husband, Pasqual, and their two sons lived in another room. Needless to say, privacy was non-existent.

The Italians were desperately poor, but basically good people. I found them affable company, although they did not keep very clean. One day, Maria confided to Sara that she feared her husband's affections were waning.

"What kind of perfume do you think I should wear?" Maria inquired, obviously thinking of a dubious solution.

Hoping to drop a broad hint for the benefit of all of us, Sara advised, "The best perfume is soap and water!"

❧

To do the washing, Sara soaked the clothes in the reddish-colored well water, then soaped the clothes and spread them in the sun on stones or on the grass. The hot sun helped bleach out the dirt. Then the clothes were rinsed and dried. I made the soap by boiling caustic soda and beef fat.

Sara and Maria gathered pieces of eucalyptus wood to use for cooking, to save money spent for fuel. When wet, the wood gave off billows of foul smelling smoke. The iron was heated on charcoal, and kerosene lamps provided the only light. The window openings, having no glass, were covered with ill-fitting wooden shutters which were no barrier to insects. The poverty and squalor of our living conditions were unnerving and frayed dispositions. Some of the utensils we brought to Americana were luxuries to the Italians, and constant borrowing provoked Sara to anger and friction with the other households.

Accustomed as we were to staying clean and comfortable with daily showers in Israel, Sara and I suffered from the lack of this facility. Inventing one became imperative.

"What can you do?" Sara implored. "This climate has to be washed off every day or we will rot out of our skins!"

"I have an idea, Sara. Bear up for a few days longer. I'm going to rig us a shower."

I brought home an empty oil barrel, and began to attach a tap to it.

"What's that for?" Vincente asked, as he observed the project underway.

"It's going to be a shower, if you don't mind if I mount this barrel on the rafters of the outhouse," I explained.

"Go right ahead," Vincente laughed. "Sounds like a good idea!"

All of the Italians watched with curiosity as I improvised the shower. After installing the barrel with the tap on the outhouse rafters, I built a platform of planks under it to cover the dirt floor. I was now ready to demonstrate the procedure. Standing on a ladder outside the building, I filled the barrel with water. Then, from inside, I opened the tap to produce a shower.

"Bravo! Bravo!" the Italians applauded in approval. "We have running water! Hurrah for our friend Adolfo!"

The Italians were delighted with the new convenience, and became ardent users of the shower.

"Convenience" was hardly an appropriate description. Carrying the water for its use was quite a chore. One shower usually required two buckets full. Often the water had to be fetched from the neighbors' well two blocks away. The neighbors, Ukrainians from Romania, were zealous Jew-haters. Their conversations were habitually sprinkled with anti-Semitic remarks. They were unaware that we were Jews, since Henry had advised us to conceal our identity as such. In compliance with my uncle's counsel, I had changed my name to Adolfo, Sara to Sonya, Nechama to Nina, and Chaim to Jaime. We told people that we were German, and I was known in Americana as the German, "o Alemon." One day, I noticed that the baker had written my name

as "Adolfo Lemon," thinking this was my real name. Lemon also
means "lemon" in Portuguese. It was rather a sour private joke to
me.

Vincente gave me a plot of ground near the house for a
garden. I planted various kinds of vegetables, including onions,
kohlrabi, cauliflower, and cabbage. A farmer at heart, I tended the
garden with great pleasure. I enjoyed being outdoors after
working all day in the stifling factory. One night, during a full
moon, I awoke and was prompted to look out the window at the
garden. To my horror, an army of huge black termites was cutting
away the leaves of the vegetables, and carrying off pieces twice
their size. Vincente had mentioned termites under the house,
and described the six-foot-high towers of clay the South
American termites build in the jungle—structures that cannot be
chipped with an axe. I stood aghast as I watched hundreds of the
voracious creatures making a trail into the woods with their prey
—my beloved vegetables! That was the end of the garden.

Since there was no ceiling in the house, every noise and
voice could be heard from all quarters. This made life often
comical, but crude as well. Pasqual had stomach troubles, and his
gastric attacks during the night were only one kind of distur-
bance. Every night's sleep was broken by grunts and groans,
snoring, or children crying. Sara despaired over our zoo-like
existence, and longed for just a shred of privacy.

"Lice! The children have lice!" she cried out in horror at the
discovery. "From playing with the Italian brood, no doubt! Those
boys also have trachoma. They are unhealthy playmates for
Nechama and Chaim. Oh, Eliezer! Get rid of the lice!"

I shaved Chaim's head, and dusted Sara and Nechama with
D.D.T. My family's circumstances grieved me deeply, but as yet,
there was no way out.

Christmas, 1954, was approaching. The two Italian families
planned to have their Christmas meal together. Maria and
Pasqual owned a duck, Iducca and Nicola, a rooster. Neither bird
was a promising treat, being scrawny and ill-fed. The rooster

once pecked little Chaim in the eye, and I threatened to kill the bird on the spot.

"No! Eliezer! Not now! Please!" Nicola pleaded. "Wait until Christmas. We will have the bird for our holiday dinner!"

I conceded to stay the execution, but now, as Christmas neared, it became apparent that neither family wanted to kill their birds. Sara and I could hear the continuous arguments over who would provide which bird, or if one should be killed at all. On Christmas Day, the argument was still unresolved, and the Italians ate potatoes and macaroni for dinner.

Working at Citra, I had no time to think. I arose at 5:00 a.m., worked until 5:00 p.m., and did chores when I came home. I was always tired. Our communal living was making a nervous wreck of Sara, and threatening the health of the children. To alleviate the grim situation, I decided to build a house of our own. I sold two gold rings and a useless osterizer to make a down payment on a lot. The items netted 1000 cruseros. I purchased what was called a "popular house plan," and presented it to city hall. The city hall controller had to be bribed to obtain a permit to live in the house. The plan was for a two-room house with a half kitchen and an outhouse. There would be no electricty or plumbing. With the help of two laborers, I built the house. The brick walls were constructed using the red, sticky, native mud as mortar. For a month, I hauled water to the site by mules.

Vincente helped put up the rafters on New Year's Day, 1955. From the ground, Vincente threw tiles up to me on the roof. One by one, the tiles were put into place. While the whole town was taking a holiday, shooting off fireworks, and celebrating the New Year, we finished the little house.

Like Poland, Brazil is predominantly Roman Catholic in religious affiliation. The churchgoing people in Americana, and even the local radio station, recited Catholic litanies so many times a day that nearly thirty years later, I could still repeat them in Portuguese. Inevitably, one day Vincente invited me to go to Mass with him.

"Adolfo, why don't you come to church with us today? It won't hurt you and might do you some good."

"No, thanks, Vincente," I declined. "I have a headache."

I did not really have a headache. I had been inside a Catholic church before. Helena customarily took Ernest and me to church on Polish holidays. The special occasions were called "exchange days." The Jewish children were taken to church, and the Catholic children went to synagogue. I remembered being repelled by all the religious ornaments, statues, incense, holy water, and mysterious ceremonies. My oldest aunt, Berta's sister Elizabeth, had converted to Catholicism. Her home was full of crucifixes, images of Christ, and the Virgin Mary, religious symbols which my people regarded as forbidden "graven images." I recalled these childhood impressions, and had no interest in accepting Vincente's invitation. I saw nothing I wanted in that kind of religion, and I had almost forgotten my father's blessing as well.

CHAPTER 13

A Ray of Light

The roof leaked in our new home. Sweeping out the water was a challenge during the rainy season. Every two months, Uncle Isadore drove in his car to Americana for a visit, and everytime he came, he found fault with something. He wanted me to be successful and prosperous, which, of course, would also relieve my two uncles of their continuing responsibility to help the Urbach family.

My working hours were long, and the wages discouragingly low. I earned 2000 cruzeros per month, half of that sum going for a house payment. But something was happening in my life that would change and dramatically redirect my future course. Shortly after my arrival at the factory, a handsome young man, with a moustache like my own, approached with a smile.

"Are you new here?" he asked amicably.

"Yes," I replied, a little suspicious of such a direct and overly-friendly demeanor.

"Where are you from?" the young man continued.

"Germany."

"Are you a Catholic?"

"No. What is wrong with being a Catholic?"

"Nothing. I was just wondering what religion you followed." The young man handed me a tract.

"I don't follow any religion." I was now warily on guard with this inquisitive stranger.

Despite my defensive reaction, the conversational assault continued.

"I noticed on your time card that you have an Old Testament name. How did you get that name?"

"I don't know. It just came about."

I definitely wanted to avoid any religious discussion, and refused to elaborate further on my real name, which had to be registered on the factory's official employee time card.

"Well, it's good to meet you," Laerte went on. "I've heard that you are European. What do you know about Communism? How is life in Europe? We don't have much contact with the outside world here in Americana. I'd like to hear your comments about these things."

The questions kept coming, and I responded to the genuine interest being shown in what I had to say. However, I did not mention that I had come from Israel, and I did not reveal that I was Jewish.

The young man's name was Laerte Modolo. His father was Italian and his mother was a third-generation American. He had dropped out of high school to support the family when his father became ill, and now Laerte was 23 years old. As our first conversation ended, Laerte shook my hand warmly, and said, "See you tomorrow, Adolfo. I'd like to get to know you better."

When Laerte left, I read the tract he had given to me. It was Christian literature, and advocated belief in Jesus Christ by the Protestant persuasion. Although my Jewishness did not mean a great deal except as a cause for being persecuted, I was not inclined to adopt a belief in the One whom rabbis and Jews for centuries had referred to as "That Man," to avoid speaking His name out of hatred.

Many brutal pogroms against the Jews had been instigated in the name of "That Man." The Jews suffered more at the hands of so-called Christians than from any other group of people. Still, I was impressed with the cordiality that Laerte showed to me. I wanted to know this fellow better, too.

Laerte and I soon became good friends. Although he had a bicycle, Laerte regularly walked several miles on the way home from work with me. He frequently shared his faith with his new friend, and explained how and why he had accepted Jesus Christ as his Lord and Savior. Laerte's enthusiasm and sincerity were appealing to me, and by contrast, I was beginning to recognize another kind of barrenness in my own life. Laerte was poor like myself, but somehow, this young man seemed strangely rich.

"Adolfo, I have some Christian friends I'd like you to meet," Laerte invited one day on our way home from the factory. "Please come to a meeting at our church next Wednesday evening. I'm sure you will enjoy the fellowship, and my friends will likewise be pleased with your company."

"Well, if your friends are anything like you, Laerte, I'm sure it would be a pleasant evening. I'll be there."

The church was Presbyterian. The first evening that I attended a meeting, the program was a film on the life of Martin Luther. It was my introduction to Protestantism. Several members of the Christian group worked at the factory, whom I already knew, and many other people went out of their way to introduce themselves, and welcome me to the meeting. They took me on a tour of the church, and eagerly showed me a German Bible in Gothic print, since I had been introduced as Adolfo from Germany. It was clear that this gesture was made from a genuine concern to please me, and not just from pride in their religious artifacts.

"Do you have a Bible?" someone asked me.

"No, I don't have a Bible."

"Then we will get you one right away!" the members promised.

During the rest of the evening, the congregation explained their beliefs to me. They told me that a person must be filled with the Holy Spirit of God in order to live a truly Christian life.

"There are many professed Christians who do not follow in the spirit of the Lord," the group counseled. "Always look to see how God's love is manifested in a believer's life. You will know the Lord's true followers by their love. Jesus' message was clear from the beginning, and was re-told many times in the New Testament."

One of the members quoted a particularly blunt passage from 1 John 4:20-21: "If anyone says, 'I love God,' and hates his brother, he is a liar; for he who does not love his brother whom he has seen, cannot love God whom he has not seen. And this commandment we have from him, that he who loves God should love his brother also."

The band of Christians, a motley mixture of several nationalities, were emphatic and unequivocal in their presentation of the Gospel of love. To the Jewish victim of hate and persecution who was receiving it, it was like manna from heaven. It meant that all Gentiles are not Christians, a common confusion among my people, and also that those who carried the Christian label, and did not love, were not living in accordance with the commandment of their Lord. "That Man" had not directed His followers to persecute the Jews. A few scales fell from my eyes.

I observed that this congregation did, indeed, seem to be on fire with the spirit of the God they professed to believe in, and they had some intangible power in their lives I had never seen before. Both the spirit and the power greatly attracted me. The faith of these people was real and spontaneous. They talked and prayed as though they **knew** God in some personal way. I attended to their prayers, (they even prayed for me), and was irresistibly drawn into the fellowship of these believers. I went to another meeting, and another.

"Senor Adolfo," a member named Silas asked me point-blank on the third evening, "do you believe in God?"

"Yes," I answered truthfully, although I knew that whatever

I believed, my faith was peripheral to my life, and I prayed only when in dire need or danger. My emergency prayers were addressed to an ambiguous Deity who was formally known as the "God of our fathers, Abraham, Isaac, and Jacob." I had no personal knowledge of, or relationship with, the God of my fathers.

"And in Jesus Christ?" Silas queried further.

I was not prepared for the question. I did not know it then, but hardly anyone is. Nor, as I remarked many times later after receiving the call to be a missionary, did I know what I was getting into with my answer. When I first read the story of Peter's confession in the New Testament, I felt a great empathy with that disciple who blurted out his reply to Jesus' question, "Who do you say that I am?" The scene in the Gospel story reminded me of the time in my own life when I was pressed to make a decision about the Messiah. From late adolescence, I had not paid much attention to religion, but as a Jew, I could not escape the aversion of my people to Christendom, and the valid reasons for it. Still, I was gifted with a comprehensive love for all kinds of people, Jew and Gentile alike, which often seemed to have nowhere to go. I had both friends and enemies among the Gentiles, but I never blanketed the friends with the sins of the enemies.

What struck me as the most odd about the present moment, was that the people in this congregation did not know that I was Jewish, nor would it have made any difference. Their only concern was that I be saved by the Lord Jesus. The universality of the Gospel message had already been driven home by their teaching, and I could no longer plead, "but I'm Jewish!" I did, in fact, sense a strange kindred spirit that transcended the mixture of nationalities present at the meeting. I felt like a prodigal son who has just been invited home. It seemed an eternity before I answered Silas.

"Yes, I am convinced that Jesus is the Messiah."

A great wave of relief, (or was it peace?), flooded my mind

and heart as I made the confession of faith. But even as the Holy Spirit convicted me of the truth about Jesus of Nazareth, I was acutely conscious of the "No" emblazoned on the pages of Jewish history for nearly 2000 years. Unaware of the wall of tradition I had just breached, the whole assembly of believers was ecstatic. Silas pumped my hand vigorously.

"If you believe in Jesus Christ, you are my brother! And since you are my brother, you should come to Sunday School. Will you come?"

"I'll come," I agreed, still astonished at the step I had taken, but eager to please my new friends.

I attended not only Sunday School, but the worship service, and mid-week prayer meetings. Sunday School fascinated me. Everyone read from the Bible, quite different from Hebrew school, where only the teacher read. The Sunday School teacher said prayers that I thought would certainly move mountains. At the prayer meetings, everybody knelt down and spoke spontaneously to God, unlike the practice of reciting from the Jewish prayer book that I was familiar with from boyhood. Soon I, too, felt the presence of this unseen Person to whom the believers prayed and called Lord.

◌

My confession of faith in the Messiah was surely not a surprise to the Lord God who declared through His spokesman that His word "is living and active, sharper than any two-edged sword, piercing to the division of soul and spirit, of joints and marrow, and discerning the thoughts and intentions of the heart." (Hebrews 4:12). Centuries earlier, the prophet Isaiah wrote of the power of God's word:

"For as the rain and the snow come down from heaven,
and return not thither but water the earth,
making it bring forth and sprout, giving seed to the sower and bread to
    the eater.
so shall my word be that goes forth from my mouth;

it shall not return to me empty, but it shall accomplish that which I
purpose, and prosper in the thing for which I sent it."
(Isaiah 55:10-11).

All through elementary school in Skoczow, I was exposed
indirectly to the Gospel. Every week, a Catholic priest, a
Lutheran pastor, and a rabbi brought their respective religious
instruction to the children in public school. Classes opened daily
with a recitation of the Lord's Prayer. During the Christmas
season, the children sang many Polish Christmas carols in
school. A nativity play, complete with a portable creche, was a
tradition in the small town. Young Catholic children traveled
around to homes, singing carols and acting out the nativity
drama. The troupe always visited our inn. My father was not
intolerant of this practice, and most of his customers were
Gentiles anyway. Fifty years later, I could still remember the
words and melodies of these Polish Christmas songs.

Another early encounter with the Christian faith occurred
when an elementary school classmate died. The whole class was
taught a hymn to sing at the boy's funeral. I remember this hymn
quite clearly.

"Where is the soul's repose?
Her peace and paradise?
Where of her wishes and hopes
Is the place of fulfillment?

"No, no, no, no, it is not a fable.
My soul's homeland
Is at heaven's gate."

The Gospel had been planted in my head very early. In time,
the message worked its way to my heart. The Presbyterians in
Americana were not really the first ones to introduce me to the
Lord Jesus. They were rather the catalysts who ignited the latent
Gospel already in my soul. God's word had accomplished the
purpose for which it was sent. The Lord had a mission for me,
and this was only the beginning.

ॐ

I became regular in attendance at church functions. I met several businessmen in the church, and went bicycling with the youth group, although I was older than most of them. The outings with such wholesome company was an immense pleasure, and Sara could not help but notice my brighter spirit. Finally, her curiosity had to be satisfied.

"Why are you so happy lately? Have you found a pot of gold somewhere?"

"My good friend Laerte is getting married Sunday in the church," I replied, evasively at first. "We're invited to the wedding, and I want you to go with me, Sara. Many of my Gentile friends will be there, and I'd like for you to meet them."

Sara was immediately apprehensive about entering a Christian church. As a child, she lived in the Ukraine, where Jews were beaten and abused by Christians at Eastertime. She vividly remembered having to hide in fear of her life during the Christian holy season. The name of Jesus still made her shudder, as it evoked those horrible memories. I knew what she was thinking before she answered.

"Come now, Sara, you will be surprised. It isn't anything like you imagine there. You'll see."

Sara reluctantly agreed to go the wedding. Her first surprise was the interior of the church. There were no crosses, no pictures, no statues, or any other Catholic trappings like the churches in Poland. The church was a simple, rustic building furnished only with wooden benches. It reminded Sara of a synagogue, and she felt comfortable in the plain surroundings. The wedding was concluded with joyful hymn-singing by the congregation. The music was appealing to Sara, and softened her fearful spirit.

After the wedding, members of the congregation introduced themselves, and some had Old Testament names. Sara began to relax and enjoy the fellowship. She attended the Sunday services thereafter, and socialized with the people at the church during the week. Gradually, the light of faith dawned in Sara's heart and mind, as her new friends continued to manifest the Lord's love to her. Following an unusual experience of Jesus' presence, Sara, too, accepted the Messiah of God. Our new-found faith and companionship were of timely benefit to our otherwise cheerless existence in Americana.

⌁

Working in the factory was too exhausting for too little reward. A Czechoslovakian named Vasco, whom I met on the boat from Israel, came to Americana for a visit. He worked as a mechanic in Sao Paulo for awhile, a rare interlude of regular employment for him. He was a soldier of fortune most of the time, and spent five years with the French Foreign Legion in Vietnam. He visited me while I was a caretaker at Rio Bonito, and now, to indulge his spirit of adventure, Vasco was on his way into the jungle to search for diamonds in the rivers. In the course of the conversation, I expressed my dissatisfaction with the factory job to my friend.

"How would you like to try a private business venture?" Vasco obviously had something in mind.

"And what would that be?" I was skeptical, but interested.

"I know a butcher and sausage maker in Sao Paulo who is looking for a partner. His name is Carlos Robel. I met Carlos in the Foreign Legion, and ran into him again recently in the city. Would you be interested into going into business with him?"

"I would consider the possibility," I agreed cautiously, thinking that an opportunity to break out of the low-paying factory job might have materialized.

Negotiations were carried out through the mobile Vasco, and a deal was made. I agreed to supply the money to start the business and provide room and board for Carlos; Carlos furnished his expertise as a master butcher to make the sausages.

Several days later, a neatly dressed Carlos arrived with his suitcases. He was a blond, husky young man, about 25 or 30 years of age. His aggressive manner suggested confidence in his business acumen, which encouraged me to proceed immediately with the plans.

"First of all," I advised, "we need to solicit financial backing from a few members of the church. I have already spoken to some of the businessmen in the congregation. One of the elders, Senor Herminio, is himself a butcher, and he has expressed interest. He and one or two others want you to demonstrate your sausage-making to see whether they like your product."

"That's very good," Carlos concurred. "I'll be happy to do that. Make the arrangements right away."

The demonstration was successful, and Senor Herminio agreed to collaborate in starting a sausage factory. I obtained a license, rented a shop and a meat grinder, and bought a sausage-filling machine. I had high hopes of becoming a successful entrepreneur.

It was not to be so. There were problems from the beginning of the venture. Carlos made the first batch of sausages, which I was to sell to the grocery shops. We soon discovered that our pure pork sausages were too expensive for the customers to buy. Some of the butchers themselves made sausages from leftover meat, which could be sold much more cheaply. With our overhead, Carlos and I were unable to compete with the lower prices. I also discovered that I had some gut level qualms about a Jew handling pork.

Although Carlos was a good butcher, he was a quarrelsome man with a violent temper, and he liked to drink. Neither was he long on scruples.

"We have to cut down our overhead to stay in business, Eliezer," Carlos calculated. "There is only one way I know to do that. The slaughter house taxes can be avoided if we go directly to the farms and slaughter our own animals. Of course, we'll need a car to bring the pork back from the farms."

I did not approve of either scheme. The first idea was illegal, and a car was too expensive.

"We don't have any money for a car," I pointed out, "and we have too much invested in the business to operate illegally."

"We have too much invested **not** to try to stay in business," Carlos countered. "Do you want to lose everything? We don't have to pay for a car all at once. We'll buy one on the installment plan."

Carlos pushed his solution argumentatively, and I was overruled. I tried to hope that Carlos's plan would salvage our floundering business. We bought a 1948 Ford that had been altered from a coupe to a truck. The car was a calamity on wheels. The radiator was rusted out, and after a few weeks, the block sprung a leak causing the oil to be mixed with water. I gave Carlos my last dollar to go to Sao Paulo to buy a used block.

Vasco was visiting us when Carlos returned home late one night. Carlos had been drinking and was very cantankerous.

"We've been in business for six months, and have made no money at all. I want to be paid wages. I'm not working for nothing anymore!" Carlos pounded his fist on the table, and glared at me through his alcohol-reddened eyes.

"We had no contract about wages," I reminded him. "I said if the business prospers, half of it would be yours. Now I'm giving you food and lodging. I'm keeping my part of the deal."

Carlos became extremely agitated, and approached me menacingly.

"You dirty Jew!" he exploded, taking a swing at my head.

The epithet and threatening gesture triggered vivid flashes of Holocaust memories. A dark tide of emotion swept through my mind, and I grabbed a knife from the wall rack. Vasco sprang between us, and wrested the knife from my hand.

"Cool off, you two! We can settle this without a fight!"

"It's no use, I'm finished with this crazy man. Get out!" I ordered Carlos. "I can't work with you any more!"

Carlos reeled out of the room, hastily collected his belongings, and commandeered the new bicycle recently bought for joint use. He also wanted to take the sausage-making machine, but I would not let him. Carlos sold the bicycle for money to go to Sao Paulo.

The sausage enterprise had gone broke in six months. I had no money, and the house was mortgaged to finance the business. I returned the sausage-filling machine in hopes of receiving some money for it, but the merchant refused to pay me until the machine sold again.

"What will I do now?" I asked Vasco in despair.

Although he had contracted malaria on his last expedition, Vasco had another plan to offer.

"I'm leaving soon to go on a diamond hunt again. Come with me. We might strike it rich this time!"

I thought the proposition over for a few minutes. It sounded wild and foolish, but no more foolish than a number of other risks I had taken to survive in the past. An incurable optimist, I went for the lucky diamond strike.

"Well, why not? There is nothing I can do here to support my family, and I'm buried in debts. I'm ready to try anything."

I left the receipt for the sausage-maker with Sara, packed my clothes, my Bible, a hunting rifle, and a fishing knife, and headed for the Brazilian interior.

CHAPTER 14

In Search of Diamonds

Campo Grande, one thousand miles into the heart of Brazil, was the last stop on the railroad line. Vasco and I rode the lumbering old wooden train for a week. From Campo Grande, we hitched a ride on a truck that was carrying gasoline drums. For three days, we slept on the truck and stopped at roadside hovels that served travelers. Other than by trucks, the interior was accessible only by small planes and barges, which transported necessary food supplies and merchandise. The roads were dangerous. Here, the "law of the jungle" was not just a descriptive phrase. Coarse men, driven by hunger and greed, committed brutal attacks upon unwary strangers. With our meager funds, Vasco and I bought bread and bananas, and paid fare to the truck driver. We were constantly hungry.

Another week later, we arrived at Cuiaba, geographical center of South America, and capital of the state of Mato Grosso, and possibly the "mosquito capital" of the world. The town was also the center of diamond, rubber, and Brazil-nut commerce. After an overnight stay in Cuiaba, we caught a ride on another truck loaded with supplies, heading for Diamantina. We rode all night and part of the next day atop the truck with a young mulatto woman who said that her husband died after being bitten by a snake while he was tapping rubber trees. She had a small child with her, and was going to look for a job in Diamantina.

A Catholic cathedral formed the skyline of the ramshackle little town of Diamantina. There was a convent in the nearby mountains. The town plaza was paved with cathead stones, a native cobblestone which made wheeled traffic clatter noisily over the street. Diamantina had once housed many slaves who were used as diamond sievers, until slavery was abolished in Brazil in 1880.

A diamond expedition was a complex affair. Those who could not afford a private trip could join a group. At least seven months in the jungle were required to make an expedition financially worthwhile. Customarily, a group was funded by a wealthy promoter who shared half of the proceeds with the workers. As might be expected among such rough fortune seekers, the workers often hid the diamonds they found, and on occasion, greed precipitated murder.

The divers wore an old-fashioned diver's suit with helmet. Air was pumped from the boat. The divers collected gravel from the bottom of the river, and sent it up in buckets. The workers on the shore sieved the gravel for diamonds. The men held three sieves, each over the other. The diamonds, if any, usually appeared in the third sieve. Supplies for such an expedition included medicines, snake serum, weapons to ward off wild animals, a boat, and food staples.

Julius the Slovak was a diamond siever who lived in Diamantina. Vasco knew the man from a previous expedition, and hoped that the fellow Czech would take the two of us in for a short while. But Julius, a tall, blue-eyed, blond man, was not happy to see the newcomers. He lived in a one-room hut with a make-shift kitchen. A small, lethargic Negro woman was his companion.

"It's too early to look for diamonds," Julius told us sullenly. "You can't dive in the river here from April to July because of high water. Come the season, if you want to look for diamonds, you'll have to go 600 leagues downriver in a boat with good supplies. And you need to find a group, a cooperative. In the meantime, you'll have to get a job. I'm living on borrowed money already and can't help you. And there's no room for you in the hut."

Vasco and I bought hammocks and stayed around Julius's place for a few days, trying to decide what to do. We were eager to get out of Julius's way.

"I worked for a jungle surveyor the last time I was out here," Vasco recalled. "We might find work with the surveying party, if we can find them."

"Do we have a choice?" I asked rhetorically. "Let's go."

We alternately hitchhiked and walked nearly 100 miles into the jungle to reach the surveyor's party. On the way, I grew so hungry, I drank water from a creek, a dangerous thing to do.

"You crazy man!" Vasco yelled. "Don't ever do that again, unless you're tired of living! You can get all kinds of terrible things from that putrid water!"

Upon our arrival at the camp, we discovered that the group was not surveying the jungle, but preparing a small landing strip for prospective buyers from Rio de Janiero and Sao Paulo. Salesman in those cities were selling tracts of jungle to investors, supposedly for colonization. Vasco and I were given a chilly reception by the Brazilians, who suspected all foreigners, but we were hired. The company had no bulldozers to clear the ground of trees and shrubs. The dense growth was tackled by men with pick axes, shovels, and saws. The workers slept in open lean-to shelters, giving mosquitos free access to them.

Every day, the men walked five miles from camp to the landing strip site. We carried food and water supplies with us. To protect my head from the hot sun, I wrapped a towel around my head and wore a hat on top of the towel. On the way to the water bucket one day, my head brushed a tree branch. Reaching up to straighten my dislodged hat, I felt something on my hand. The something was a gigantic black spider, a shocking sight. I shook my hand vigorously, but the tarantula clung, its large hairy body covering the entire back of my hand. I picked up the shovel I had dropped and scraped the spider off with it. As the underbrush was being cleared for the landing site, these ominous creatures sought the trees. Although the bite of the tarantula is painful, it is not significantly poisonous to human beings. I was thankful that I was not bitten in any case, but the experience was so unnerving, I began to pray daily for deliverance from the jungle and a safe reunion with my family.

After two months in the jungle, the food supplies for the work party were used up. The foreman broke camp, and ordered most of the workers to leave. Vasco fell ill with malaria attacks shortly after our arrival, and had to go back to Diamantina for medical treatment. He returned just before the camp ran out of supplies, still unable to work. The unsympathetic foreman had declared, no work—no food. Both Vasco and I were glad to leave and began the long, hazardous trip back to Cuiaba via Diamantina.

Destitute and ravenously hungry, we stopped at a crossroads inn where a mulatto man sold food and whiskey.

"Can we do some work for you in exchange for food and lodging?" Vasco inquired of the proprietor.

"Yes, there is work to be done here," the man replied. "I'm going to move off this place soon, and my fields of corn, rice, and beans need to be harvested. I could use your help."

The mulatto informed us that two padres were coming in a couple of weeks to baptize his daughter's baby, and invited us to attend the ceremony.

When the padres arrived, they held confession and Mass, in which Vasco and I declined to participate, but we did go to vespers. The padres offered each of us a religious medallion and a rosary. I accepted the gifts as symbols of the faith I was struggling to keep alive unaided in a coarse environment.

The padres were on their way to Cuiaba, and offered to take

Vasco and me with them. At another crossroad stop, I overheard some diamond field hands and plantation workers talking about "the Jew" who lived in Cuiaba.

"We may be in luck, Vasco. If there is an influential Jew in Cuiaba, I'm sure he will help us."

"You guys are a marvel," Vasco laughed. "What a network you keep!"

During the trip to Cuiaba, I began to have fever black-outs.

A traditional promenade was in progress on the town plaza when we arrived. Every Saturday night after work, the village boys stood in a cluster while the girls paraded around them, preening themselves and giggling with adolescent frivolity. I was not interested in this native custom. I was listening intently to conversation to hear word of "the Jew." I heard someone call out.

"Hey! Czecho!"

Approaching the Czech man, I asked,

"Who is the Jew everybody talks about?"

"Don't you know? He's the richest man in town—made a fortune in diamonds, airplanes, land holdings, and gambling."

"Where can I find him?"

"You can't miss his place," Czecho said. "It's that big house at the end of town. If you are a friend of his, tell him that I, Czecho, sent you!" Czecho laughed raucously at his own joke.

Vasco decided his fortune still lay in the diamond field, and left to drive a truck back into the jungle with another friend, leaving me to seek out the Jew. The man, a Hungarian, was not at home when I knocked at the door. The Brazilian wife came to answer the knock, and I introduced myself in German.

"You are European?" the attractive, dark-haired woman responded.

"Yes, I am from your husband's part of the world. I would like to see him if I may."

"He is not at home right now, but I expect him in a few

minutes. Please come in and wait for him," the wife invited.

The house was luxuriously furnished, a sharp contrast to anything I had seen for a long time. The hostess, Mrs. Greenblatt, offered me some cold juice, and made me feel comfortable in the surroundings.

Mr. Greenblatt entered almost immediately, and was cordial to his unexpected guest. He listened with interest as I explained my circumstances.

"So right now you need a job, eh?" the Jew said encouragingly. "I'll introduce you to a fellow Hungarian here who owns several shops and a bus line. I'm sure he can find something for you to do."

The fellow Hungarian, a Gentile, hired me to oversee the operation of the bus line, and I was pleased with the new job. I attended the little Presbyterian church in Cuiaba, and got acquainted with the members. Happily, I wrote a letter to Sara to tell her the good news. The response was a telegram from Uncle Isadore, informing me that Sara wanted to go back to Israel. The telegram ended: COME HOME IMMEDIATELY.

Following the telegram, Isadore called me at my hotel room in Cuiaba.

"I'm sending you a plane ticket for Sao Paulo, nephew. Use it at once! You are needed at home."

"I have a job here, Uncle Isadore. How can I leave? What is the trouble? Is someone ill in my family?"

"No one is ill, but you must come at once," Isadore insisted, and hung up the telephone.

Fully expecting to return to my job after I found out what the urgent matter was at home, I asked for a short leave of absence. My employer agreed, and even bought me a bus ticket back from Sao Paulo.

The date was May 1, 1956, when I arrived in Sao Paulo, thin and drawn. Only Isadore was waiting at the station. He took us to a restaurant and ordered a big meal for me.

"Where are Sara and the children? Why aren't they here?

Sara wrote that she had moved, but didn't say where to. Where did she move to?"

"How should I know? Am I the husband?" Isadore jibed. "I will not tell you where Sara and the children are unless you do as I say."

Isadore's demand was adamant, and confused me.

"Do what? What is it you are saying?"

"Take a train to Rio and go to the Israeli consulate. Ask for a re-entry permit to Israel. Here is your passport."

I stared wearily at Isadore. I was seriously ill, still broke, and tired of the struggle to live in Brazil. The black passport lying on the table before me symbolized my dismal failure in another country. My vision blurred. I picked up the document and blinked to clear my eyes. My uncle was already waiting impatiently at the door of the restaurant.

Isadore put me on a night train to Rio de Janiero. In the morning, I went to the Israeli consulate and asked for a re-entry permit to Israel.

"Why do you want to return to Israel?" the official asked.

"I am an Israeli. I want my children to be educated in Israel."

The permit was granted with no further questions. That afternoon, I took the plane back to Sao Paulo. Isadore met me and escorted me to the travel bureau where he bought boat tickets for the whole family. I was in no position to argue with my uncle. I still did not know where Sara and the children were staying. After the boat tickets were purchased, Isadore took me to a hotel.

"Sara and the children are here," he announced. "Go find them."

Isadore let me out of the car and drove off.

The reunion with my family in Sao Paulo was mixed with joy and bitterness.

"You look very good, Sara. You have a new hairdo. Very nice. How did you manage? When did you come to Sao Paulo? That's a pretty new dress. The children! They've grown a little, haven't they? Tell me what you've been doing. I'm sorry I was gone for so long. It must have been difficult for you."

"If you'll stop with the questions, I'll tell you what we've been doing for three months," Sara interrupted my apologetic barrage.

"Shortly after you left, I moved us to an apartment in Americana, and sold the furniture to pay the rent. The car, of course, was repossessed—just as well, I couldn't drive it anyway. Then, praise God, the sausage-making machine sold, and I collected several hundred dollars. I put most of it away in safe-keeping, and invested some of the money in skirts and blouses to sell for a little income. Our church friends helped out whenever I needed something, and Uncle Isadore watched over us all the time. I prayed a lot, and the Lord graciously assured me of His divine guidance and protection. We managed pretty well, although it wasn't easy, and we missed you. Isadore brought us here to meet you."

"You did valiantly, Sara! I'm proud of your resourcefulness. I admit going into the jungle was not a good way to try to solve our problems. Please forgive this unfortunate episode. We'll go back to Israel now and start over."

Nechama was nine years old, a chubby little blond girl who spoke Portuguese well after two years in Brazilian schools. Chaim was a solemn but energetic five-year-old who had just started school. To my great anguish, Chaim did not recognize his father. I vowed never to leave my family again, no matter how destitute our financial situation.

We stayed a week in the hotel room after my return, waiting for the ship to depart. In June, we left Sao Paulo for the port of Santos to board the ship. The crossing was a miserable time for me. I had a temperature of 104 degrees, and was delirious. In the little ship hospital, the doctor could not diagnose the disease. Only when we transferred to an Israeli ship in Marseilles did I realize what the ailment was. While reading in the ship's library, my lower jaw began to shake beyond control, an unmistakeable sign of malaria. The malaria pills in the ship's pharmacy were moldy. Malaria had long been eradicated in Israel, and apparently was no longer an expected medical contingency. In the clutches of the dread South American disease, I once again touched the soil of the Jewish homeland.

CHAPTER 15

Jesus the Messiah

Life was complicated the first year back in Israel. Sara's mother took a taxi to Haifa, and greeted her travel-worn family as we disembarked from the ship. Again, we moved into her small, two-room apartment in Ramat Gan. We were so over-crowded, everyone's nerves soon became frayed. The clinic doctors gave me intra-muscular injections for malaria that were extremely painful. I sought a private doctor who treated me with pills. I had four malaria attacks before the disease subsided.

I was too humiliated to go back to my old job as an army accountant. I had gone out to conquer the world, to find peace in Brazil, and now I was back in defeat. My brother-in-law, Samuel, understood my reluctance to face former fellow workers, and found me a job at the Tnuva dairy on the outskirts of Tel Aviv. The work was hard physical labor, carrying boxes of milk bottles, washing them in the automat, filling them with milk, and transporting them to the freezer.

During the first six weeks on the job, I had to work extra-long hours since most of the employees had been called into the army for the 1956 Sinai War. I was exempt from military duty as were all those of recent arrival in Israel. Much of my work time was spent wheeling boxes of milk bottles in and out of the dairy freezer. Still sick and always cold, I had one bad malaria attack while in the freezer. I prayed that the Lord would deliver me from this job.

One Saturday afternoon, a car drove up in front of the apartment. A sergeant major in the Israeli army got out and reported to me.

"The colonel wants to see you right away, Urbach."

"What about?"

"He'll tell you when you get there."

On the way to meet the colonel, I imagined all sorts of reasons why I had been summoned. A number of summons I had received during my lifetime had turned out to be mixed blessings. This one was no different.

The Sinai campaign had begun a week before, and thousands of tons of munitions had to be brought from the Negev. The army was retreating to its previous positions, being threatened, not by the enemy, but by economic and political sanctions imposed by John Foster Dulles, the Secretary of State of the United States. Consequently, a great amount of paperwork—classifying, ordering, storing mortars, rifles, and machine guns—needed to be done. The army was swamped with the task, and since I was experienced in this area, the colonel wanted to reinstate me at headquarters. Former army friends urged me to come back, and I accepted the position.

The wages were better and the physical strain considerably less than at the dairy. I was happier there and on good terms with the army personnel. However, working for the army, on a war-time basis, in a Jewish state, all weighed against my faith. I was still a new believer, and my confession of faith in Jesus as the Messiah was made in a much different situation. For a long time, I had been without the solid support of other believers, and I knew my commitment had weakened.

Finding a Christian fellowship in Israel was difficult for us. There were no advertisements, no open outreach. Such things were too antagonistic in a Jewish state. A Russian friend advised me to attend the Anglican church in Jaffa, which had Sabbath evening services. I went there one Saturday, but to my disappointment, the service was quite formal, and I could not identify with the people. The clergyman wore a robe, and there were prayer books in the pews along with the hymn books. The order of worship was reminiscent of synagogue practice, which lacked the spontaneity to hold my interest.

After the service, I asked some church members where to find an informal group of believers. Batya, a kindergarten teacher at the Anglican day school, answered my request.

"There is a group of Russian believers in Tel Aviv. I think you might find what you are looking for in their fellowship. The most important thing is that they are born-again believers. Go and introduce yourself there."

The group was called Christians Assembled in the Name of the Lord. My first impression was not favorable because there were few Jews there. The leader of the group, Solomon Ostrovsky, was out of the country at the time. I attended a few meetings, then lost interest.

Salim, an Arab member of the Assembly, who had a genuine love for the Jewish people, told Ostrovsky about my brief attendance when the leader arrived back in Israel. One Friday, when I returned home from work, I found two people sitting in the apartment talking to Sara.

"This is Mr. and Mrs. Solomon Ostrovsky," Sara introduced us.

"I've heard good things about you people," I greeted them.

"We're sorry we missed your arrival in Israel," Mr. Ostrovsky began. "We have been in England the past year. Salim told us about you and Sara. You have been missed at the meetings. Is there a problem we could help you with now?"

I responded immediately to the warm nature of Mr. Ostrovsky, and was ready to confide in him.

"Well, yes, there is. I appreciate your concern. Frankly, Mr.

Ostrovsky, I do have some problems that I would like to discuss with you."

"I would be most happy to help if I can. Let's take a walk."

As we strolled around the neighborhood together, I confessed that my commitment to the Lord needed to be strengthened.

"I'm afraid I have nearly lost my faith, Mr. Ostrovsky. I don't feel the same here as I did at first in Brazil, and it's very difficult for me at work. I'm under heavy pressure to be as I was before I accepted Jesus as my Messiah, you understand? How shall I persevere in the faith under such conditions?"

Mr. Ostrovsky was sympathetic and responsive.

"We all understand that for sure, Eliezer. You aren't alone in the struggle. We have all been tempted to backslide at one time or another. We need the support of one another constantly to stay strongly committed to the Lord. Take heart, you will overcome your doubts and fears. Come back to the Fellowship and learn how to grow in the Lord!"

I was relieved to have someone to counsel and encourage me. From then on, Sara, the children, and I attended the meetings faithfully. We became part of the family of believers, and had fellowship with the group four times a week, twice on Saturday, once on Sunday, and again on Wednesday. Through the love and understanding of others, my love for the Lord became real and strong once more. I grew in the knowledge of the Lord, and in my commitment to Jesus the Messiah. I learned to walk with God through daily Bible study and prayer, and found the Lord's grace sufficient to live a Christian life.

Membership in the group fluctuated as people came and went. Among the permanent members, there was Dr. Yuk, a medical doctor and Bible teacher. He, as well as Solomon Ostrovsky, accepted Jesus as their Lord and Savior at an early age, during a revival in Russia. Ostrovsky was rejected by his family after he made his faith known to them. Abraham Yurewicz was a

Catholic who converted to Judaism. Then his wife found the Messiah, and seeing a change in her, he re-affirmed faith in Jesus. Yasha, a Russian who had a Jewish wife, overcame a long-standing drinking problem when he accepted Jesus as his Messiah. Yasha was a radiant witness in the laundry shop which he operated. Batya, the woman who told me about the group, was in poor health, but glowed with spiritual strength. Her missionary father had been killed by the Nazis in Romania. Mrs. Dosek, the grandmother of the group in her 80's, had brought up five daughters and a son in the faith. One daughter was married to Ostrovsky. There was a sweet fellowship among Jews and Arabs in the meetings.

The Assembly met in Dr. Yuk's clinic on Wednesday nights for Bible study and prayer. After the Bible study, we knelt on little cushions over the hard mosaic stone floor and prayed, in Russian, Yiddish, Hebrew, Romanian, and Arabic. There were many languages, one spirit.

My growth in the faith was a gradual and slow process. I had to overcome many traditional Jewish objections which I had inherited, and discover for myself the misrepresentations of Christianity that keep many Jewish people from considering Jesus of Nazareth the fulfillment of Israel's messianic hope and prophetic vision. I also came to understand that second-born believers in the Jewish Messiah love and respect God's first-born people, Israel, and that true believers cannot be held responsible for ecclesiastical sins, nor for the perversity ever latent in human hearts.

CHAPTER 16

Persecution

The whole Urbach family went out to the Christian fellowship meetings three or four times a week. Sara's mother and Samuel were curious to know where we were going so often, but said nothing. Curiosity turned to alarm when we all disappeared for a whole week, attending a Vacation Bible School in Jerusalem. On the way home, Sara and I left the children with the Ostrovskys in Jaffa, for a recreational visit after school. When we returned without Nechama and Chaim, Mrs. Leiner and Samuel feared the worst. They suspected that we had given the children over to a missionary boarding school. Samuel went on a frantic search to every such establishment in the area.

At 7:00 p.m., Samuel found me visiting at a Russian neighbor's house. Ignoring the man who answered the door, Samuel called out past him to address me sharply.

"Eliezer! I want to talk to you immediately!"

It was Sabbath, and Samuel was 15 kilometers from home. I knew right away that something was wrong. I left with my agitated brother-in-law, and we sat down on a bench in front of the Great Synagogue.

"Tell me the truth, and nothing else save the truth, Eliezer. Have you become a notzree (Christian)?"

"I was born a Jew, and I will die a Jew, Samuel. But I have accepted the Messiah," I answered firmly.

"I don't care what religion you embrace, but don't you dare put that poison into your children's minds! If you continue to do so, you will be unfit Jewish parents, and we will have to see what we can do about that," Samuel threatened. He was a lawyer by profession.

"Do you want us to move out of mother's apartment?"

"No, she is alone. Stay for the time being. Now let's go home and see what my sister has to say about this crazy thing!"

The Sabbath candles were lighted when we entered the apartment, glowing peace that was about to be shattered. Samuel immediately confronted his sister.

"What do you say, Sara? You haven't betrayed us, too, have you?"

"I have accepted the Messiah," Sara replied calmly. "And it's time for you also to think about it. It's five minutes to twelve on the clock of history. The Messiah might come any time, and you will be left behind!"

Samuel was horrified. By traditional interpretation, "conversion" to Christianity annihilated Jewish identity.

"How could this have happened in **our** family? Do you know what you have done? The relatives will not tolerate such a thing! This is ruinous! We cannot compromise with this terrible situation. This is the end! I don't want to associate with you any more!"

Still shouting in his burst of anger, Samuel left the apartment, slamming the door behind him.

Sara's mother was equally shocked by the news.

"Why didn't you wait until after I died?" she moaned, rocking her head in her hands. "How can we bear this humiliation?" She was grief-stricken and inconsolable.

The rest of the relatives also ostracized us. For a long time, we were not invited to any family gatherings, Passovers, bar mitzvahs, or weddings. We were particularly heartbroken over being excluded from Passovers. The believers took us into their homes at Passover, where we prayed, sang hymns, and had chicken soup and matzo balls. For many months, when Samuel came to visit his mother, he refused to speak to any of us. Sara's mother begged us not to talk about our faith to the neighbors. Family relationships became unbearably strained and unpleasant. The intolerance and rejection only served to drive us into a closer reliance upon the Lord. We kept quiet, but there was no peace at home.

The children were cautioned not to speak of Jesus at school. Nechama and Chaim were considered "different" among their peers, although for some unknown reason. Chaim was approaching Bar Mitzvah age, and feared that his friends would ask him when his Bar Mitzvah would take place. He did not know how to answer the question. As with the children of other Jewish believers, the boy's fear was palpable, but went unspoken.

At Nechama's thirteenth birthday party, her Aunt Malkah, Samuel's wife, brought her a gift. When Malkah handed the present to Nechama, I noticed that she also pressed something else into Nechama's hand. I followed my daughter out of the room, and asked Nechama for the note she had received from Aunt Malkah. The handwritten greeting read:

> I wish you all the best on your birthday, Nechama. Your parents took a step in a direction which is foreign to us. Remember that you are a daughter of Israel, and of Israel's faith.
>
> Your loving Aunt,
> Malkah

Jewish believers lived on the edge of fear and disaster. There were so few of us in Israel, we all knew one another, and quickly learned of the consequences that befell our members when they were found out—firing from a job, eviction from an apartment, harassment from the Orthodox religious community. Freedom of religion, although constitutionally guaranteed in Israel, did not extend to Hebrew Christians.

In 1957, I was baptized in the Sea of Jaffa by Solomon Ostrovsky, renewing my confession of faith. It was early spring, and the water was cold. It was like a dream to me. Fifteen or twenty other believers who attended my baptism were singing, "Oh happy day! Jesus took my sins away!" As I came forth from the water, the words of the Gospel hymn rang in my ears, and I knew that I was Messiah's man, whatever the cost. Following the ceremony, I took my first communion. Abraham Yurewicz asked me to pray. To my great joy, I prayed spontaneously in Hebrew, which I had never been able to do before. All my previous prayers had been either in Portuguese or Polish. On this day, my Jewish identity and my Messianic faith were united, preparing me to meet troublesome accusations of betrayal in the future.

Several months later, Sara was baptized. Then Nechama, now a slender teen-ager, was also baptized in the Mediterranean Sea, upon her confession of faith. The Fellowship held a "Bar Mitzvah" party for Chaim, honoring his attainment of Jewish manhood at age thirteen. At the time, Jewish believers were caught between religious traditions, not knowing which forms we should retain from our Jewish heritage, and which practices might be inappropriate to our Christian persuasion. The modern Hebrew Christian movement has since clarified many of these issues for followers of Jesus.

ॐ

Ostrovsky was to leave again for England and Canada, and consulted with me before his departure.

"I would like you to take over leadership of the group during my two-year absence," he requested. "You are my logical replacement, considering the extent of your involvement in the work, and the respect you have earned among the members of the Assembly. I'm sure that the Fellowship will grow and prosper under your able leadership, and I would feel at ease with you in charge. What do you say?"

"I would be happy to fill in for you, Solomon. You do me a

great honor, and I'm grateful for the opportunity to serve the Lord in this way. I'll do my best to keep the Fellowship going and growing while you are gone. We will miss you very much here."

Being understandable in English and fluent in Hebrew, I had been contributing to the services by translating the sermons. Active in other ways, and being known for my enthusiastic witness to the Lord, Ostrovsky concluded that I was the best candidate for his replacement. The believers needed constant encouragement. Hebrew Christians were called "meshumed," apostates. Religious politicians tried to collect money from abroad to fight the "apostates." Witnessing in public could be punished by imprisonment. We were patriotic Israeli citizens, and found the discrimination against us hard to bear.

In 1961, Dr. Daniel Fuchs, General Secretary of the American Board of Missions to the Jews, arrived in Jaffa to attend a meeting of Messianic believers, and to hire a Jewish candidate for full-time missionary service in Israel. Rachmiel Frydland, who was with the Hebrew-Christian Alliance in Israel, introduced me to Dr. Fuchs at the meeting.

"Dr. Fuchs, I would like you to meet Eliezer Urbach, a brother who is with Solomon Ostrovsky's Fellowship."

"I'm glad to meet you, Brother Urbach," Dr. Fuchs said cordially. "How are you doing here? Rachmiel has told me that you are originally from Poland. How long have you been in Israel? Do you have a family?"

As I answered his initial inquiries, Dr. Fuchs became very interested in my background and work in the Fellowship. The following day was Easter Sunday.

"I'm scheduled for a tour of Jerusalem tomorrow," Dr. Fuchs remarked, at the end of our brief conversation. "A Jewish brother is escorting me around the city. Would you like to join us?"

"I'd be delighted to do that. Thank you for inviting me. I accept with pleasure, Dr. Fuchs."

"Fine! We'll meet you on the train then. We'll begin our tour by attending the service at the Presbyterian church in Jerusalem."

Since it was mid-Passover season, the buses were over-crowded, and the train was jam-packed with holiday travelers. Orthodox Jews do not work during the half-holiday, and the train was crowded with Oriental Jews from Bukhara, Persia (Iran), Morocco, and other countries. The throng was so great, I could not reach Dr. Fuch's party until the train arrived in Jerusalem. During the three-hour trip, I prayed fervently that I would not miss the meeting with Dr. Fuchs. The General Secretary had so impressed me with his spiritual maturity and grace-filled personality, he immediately became a paragon of the man of faith that I hoped to become in time.

At the Jerusalem station, I hurriedly made my way through the exiting passengers to Dr. Fuchs. We exchanged greetings and mutual apologies for the missed connection on the train.

"Dr. Fuchs, there are no restaurants open today because of the holiday. I've brought plenty of matzo brie from home for lunch. It's not a sumptuous feast, but I'd like to share it with you."

"Matzo brie would be a fine lunch, Eliezer. My mother used to make it at home. I haven't had any for years and I would enjoy the treat."

After lunch, we combined a tour of the city and getting acquainted with one another. Dr. Fuchs was interested in learning more about my background, my wartime experiences, when and how I found the Messiah, and what I had been doing in Israel the past few years. My distinguished new friend was formulating a future for me with the American Board of Missions to the Jews, as he listened intently to my testimony.

I learned that Dr. Fuchs was a child of the Mission's original work in New York. He was a second-generation Jewish believer, his mother having been brought to the Lord by a co-worker of the founder of ABMJ, Leopold Cohn.

"My mother scrubbed floors to put me through Bible school," Dr. Fuchs told me. "Her devotion to the Lord was an enduring inspiration to me. I was led to start a photography and camera club for Jewish boys in Brooklyn, and to my great joy, many of those boys became believers, some even missionaries."

Dr. Fuchs explained the work of the American Board of Missions to the Jews to me.

"The organization was founded in 1894 by Rabbi Leopold Cohn soon after he came to know Jesus as his Messiah, in response to God's call. Since then, the ABMJ has expanded to be the most extensive world-wide outreach of any work of its kind, dedicated primarily to sharing the good news of salvation with God's covenant people." (The organization is now known as Chosen People Ministries.)

Dr. Fuchs and I spent the day together, and returned to Tel Aviv by train that evening. By this time, a deep and lasting friendship had been struck between us.

"Do you have a call to missionary service?" Dr. Fuchs asked me before the train reached Tel Aviv.

I flinched at the thought. My answer came almost immediately.

"Not now, Dr. Fuchs. I'm not ready for that yet!"

The word "missionary" had an ugly connotation in Israel. The Orthodox Jews called missionaries "soul snatchers." Peter Gutkind, the Israeli whom Dr. Fuchs came to hire, had paid a high price for being a missionary. The ultra-Orthodox rabbinical students laid siege to his house for ten days, keeping the Gutkind family prisoners in their own home. When they escaped, the family was kept from being mobbed by the intervention of non-religious Jews. Other believers had been beaten and harassed, including Solomon Ostrovsky. The Ostrovsky's child was overturned in a baby buggy and the family mobbed. Anonymous threatening letters, written by Torah activists, were sent to people for even associating with believers. The thought of being a missionary definitely did not appeal to me at the time Dr. Fuchs first planted the idea.

As we parted, Dr. Fuchs said, "Well, pray about it, Eliezer. There is a place for you at ABMJ."

"I will, Dr. Fuchs," I promised, "and thank you for your confidence in me."

The question of whether to be or not to be a missionary occupied my thoughts and prayers for the next several years. Meanwhile, Dr. Fuchs kept in touch with me, and sent a number of people to visit me in Israel.

We moved out of Grandmother Leiner's apartment and into an apartment of our own where we could practice our faith in peace. Athough I was still working for the army, life in Israel was not easy. Low wages and high taxes made it difficult to exist on a medium salary. The army job began to weigh heavily on my conscience. I was issuing millions of rounds of munitions in this position, and I no longer believed I was in the right place. I conveyed these feelings to Solomon Ostrovsky, who had returned from abroad temporarily.

"Dispensing instruments of death is incompatible with my Christian faith," I confided to my mentor. "What shall I do about it?"

"I understand the way you feel," Ostrovsky sympathized, "and we will all pray for a solution. However, you know how hard it is to find work in Israel, and your present job is providing bread for your family. My advice is to stay with it until something else materializes."

For more than two years, Sara and I prayed for God's leading. At one point, a Hebrew Christian in Cleveland, Ohio, sent us an immigration affidavit, but the quota system would keep us waiting for three years. We continued to pray.

During this time, our desire to serve God became intense, and we were getting positive inklings that we should become witnesses to our own people. We also wanted the freedom to

worship as we pleased, without fear of persecution. Aside from
frequent degradation in the press, missionaries were harassed by
anti-mission elements aimed at ending missionary activity
among the Jews. Jesus was referred to as "Yeshu," a derogatory
acronym which meant, "may his name and memory be blotted
out." Relatives of Hebrew Christians would "sit shiva," the
mourning period for the dead. Jewish believers were forced to
conceal their faith to be safe and to protect their families. I saw a
Bible bookstore burned and destroyed. Mission school windows
were broken out. A rabbi would not marry Hebrew Christians.
Couples wishing to be married had to go to Cyprus. The other
tensions and hardships inherent to life in Israel were tolerable.
The lack of religious freedom was not.

In the summer of 1963, a friend informed me that the
Canadian consulate was accepting immigrants and issuing visas
for immigration. I went to the consulate immediately. After
filling out a preliminary questionnaire, an official interviewed
me.

"You may go to Canada alone right now," the man told
me.

"But I have a family, a wife and two children."

"I'm sorry, sir, but unless you have a sponsor in Canada, you
cannot take your family."

"I don't want to divide my family. I can't go alone."

I was disappointed, but I had vowed never to leave my
family again, after the jungle episode in Brazil.

"We'll get in touch with you if anything changes," the
interviewer concluded.

Under the "religion" section on the questionnaire, I had
written that I was a Hebrew Christian. A few days later, someone
from the consulate called and asked Sara to explain what a
Hebrew Christian was.

"We are Jews who follow Christ," Sara informed the
caller.

Nonplussed, the man mumbled a thank you, and hung up.

Four weeks passed. We kept praying. A letter came from the consulate once again asking me if I were willing to go to Canada alone. I went to the consulate and told the authorities that I was still interested, but would not leave my family behind.

"Do you have any friends in Canada who would sponsor you? Perhaps someone who owns a business or is engaged in a profession?" the immigration official asked.

Solomon Ostrovsky! He was back in Canada then. Not being a resident, Ostrovsky could not sponsor us, but he might know someone who would. I wrote to Ostrovsky and explained the situation. Ten days later, I received a recommendation signed by a Ukrainian Christian who owned a delicatessen in Toronto. The man agreed to sponsor me, whom he did not know, because thirty years before, a Jew in Poland had loaned him some money, and in this way he was repaying the debt. His signature meant that the whole Urbach family could immigrate to Canada. Our prayers had been answered.

I quit my job with the army a week before the ship was to leave Israel. By faith, and with very little money, we departed for Canada. Upon our arrival in Toronto, we had dinner with the man who had sponsored us. He gave us twenty-five dollars, and welcomed us on Canadian soil.

Two days after arriving in Toronto, I found a job as an orderly at Toronto General Hospital. The wages were low, but I was able to make a down payment on a small house. For the first time since we married, the Urbachs settled down to a normal, peaceful life.

The Ostrovskys introduced us to members of the Plymouth Brethren church. The congregation held strict practices, but they had a lively faith in the Lord, and were evangelistic in outreach. I met many missionaries in the group, and asked myself what they had that the Lord had not given me. I also had a great love for people, and a desire to share the gift of salvation.

"If I have as much as they have, why don't I use it?" The question recurred in my mind and grew more insistent as time passed. I began to study the Bible diligently despite the fatigue after work, and read books on the operation of missions. The Lord's hand on my life was now being felt as a tangible pressure. A definite calling was not too far in the future.

Meanwhile, at the hospital where I worked as an orderly on the night shift, I began to share my faith in Jesus the Messiah. An immigrant from Spain who worked with me, said bluntly, "If you believe in Jesus, you are no longer a Jew."

"That is not correct," I replied in Spanish. "I am still a Jew, and I will show you that this is true from the Bible."

"I don't read English," the Spaniard put me off.

"Then I will get you a Bible in the Spanish language," I persisted, and did so immediately.

A week or so later, a Christian gentleman on the hospital staff approached me.

"Jose Valenciago, the Spanish immigrant, has steadfastly refused to take either a Bible or Christian tracts from me ever since he has been here. Now, suddenly, I see him reading a Bible you gave to him. What is your secret? How did you get him to do that?"

"The secret," I grinned, "is on the tip of the tongue. I spoke to him in his native language, and the Bible is a Spanish translation."

This "secret" continued to be a providential qualification for the Lord's service. Fluent in nine languages, my linguistic skills became instruments for telling the good news to many people. "And how is it that we hear (the Gospel), each of us in his own native language?" Acts 2:8. The gift of languages enabled me to touch numerous lives that began elsewhere than in North America. Any language represents the soul of a people, and a mother tongue is always music to the ears. I learned to sing the song of salvation in many tongues, one of the blessings that came out of my years of wandering.

Through the years from my first arrival in Israel, I corresponded with Helena. My boyhood nanny had managed to collect the Urbach family's silverware and down bedding from the inn after Nazis took the people away to Auschwitz. Helena wrote to me in Israel, asking if she should send the items to me. I instructed her to sell the silverware and bedding and keep the money for herself. Instead, Helena gave everything to the church in return for continual votive lights for me, the lone survivor of her beloved family Urbach.

While in Canada, I received the last letter from Helena before she died.

> God's blessing, dear Eliezer. I am sending heartfelt greetings to all of you. How are you? Are you healthy? Here it's very hot. No rain, very dry, nothing grows. Have you planted anything? Take care that nothing happens because you may face danger. They (the Polish underground) have murdered a (Communist) foreman in the factory. I do not know what you are doing (for a living). Be well. I greet you with God.

I am certain that Helena's life-long devotion to my physical and spiritual welfare had something to do with the shape of my destiny.

Having heard of my qualifications and experience in Israel from Dr. Fuchs, the American Board of Missions to the Jews sent a representative from their New York headquarters to ask me to come to work for them as a missionary.

"I appreciate the offer very much," I declined, "but I'm still not prepared to give you a positive answer. I'll have to wait for a definite call into that service. I don't want to uproot my newly-settled family without being certain that becoming a full-time missionary is God's will for me."

"We understand that," the representative agreed, "and you are wise to wait for a call. As you know, the Mission's work is demanding, and requires a firm commitment. We are eager to have you on our staff whenever you feel led to join us, and will keep in touch with you."

I wrestled in prayer for a resolution to my indecision, and refused a second request from the ABMJ in the meantime. I continued to feel inadequate to the task, and waited for some guidance or inner conviction that would lead me in the right direction.

In 1964, while working full-time, I enrolled in courses at Toronto Bible College. I became an avid student of the Bible, and the Holy Scriptures deepened both my faith and my commitment to the Lord. In a course on the Old Testament, the instructor gave an inspired presentation of the whole redemption drama as it unfolded from the beginning with God's selection of the Hebrew people as His chosen instruments. At last, I was convinced that the message of salvation must be taken to the Jews as well as to the Gentiles. It became clear that the divinely appointed mission of my own people was still intact. "Salvation is from the Jews," Jesus of Nazareth told the Samaritan woman at the well. At the same time, he identified Himself as the Messiah, the mediator of that salvation (John 4:22-26).

Then the apostle Paul spoke to me out of the Scriptures: "But how are men to call upon him in whom they have not believed? And how are they to believe in him of whom they have never heard? And how are they to hear without a preacher? And how can men preach unless they are sent? As it is written, 'How beautiful are the feet of those who preach good news!' " (Romans 10:14-15).

A third time, in 1967, another representative from ABMJ came to Toronto to recruit me as a missionary with their organization. On this occasion, I was certain that I should answer the call to go to New York.

CHAPTER 17

Across the Last Bridge

Although we were settled in a comfortable home, and were happy in our fellowship with the church, accepting the call from the ABMJ meant selling the house and moving again, this time to the U.S.A. We knew that missionary life would be tenuous and difficult, but we were willing to pay the price to do the Lord's will.

Before we left Toronto, Chaim was baptized at Glebemount Chapel. Nechama, now a young adult, elected to stay in Canada to determine her own life's calling. She met her husband there, and eventually they went to live in Israel.

We sold our house in the summer of 1967, and loaded up the furniture to go to New York. I was forty-six years old, and had several years of pastoral work experience with the Assembly in Israel, with which the ABMJ was familiar. The Board members also knew that I had waited a long time for a clear call into Jewish mission work, and they were satisfied that I understood the seriousness of the commitment. I looked forward to associating with dedicated men who carried on a ninety-year-old tradition in reaching out to the Lost Sheep of the House of Israel.

Sara and I had a textbook image of America as the land of the free and beautiful democracy. Untrampled by marching foreign armies, with all important freedoms constitutionally guaranteed, and 4000 miles from shore to shore, America was a legendary country to immigrants like ourselves. Could it actually be happening that this last "bridge" we were crossing, with all our worldly belongings in tow, would take us into the United States of America?

On the way to New York, my mind whirled alternately over the prospects of becoming an American citizen, and the new career I had chosen to follow in yet another new land. I prayed I would be worthy of the opportunities that Providence had sent on my path.

I began the required one year of missionary training in New York with three other missionary candidates: Mo Mogensen of New York, a Danish engineer and Bible college graduate; Arthur Katz, a teacher, and Martin Klayman, a former New York fireman. Although I had learned English mostly "by ear," I applied myself to the new program with great enthusiasm, and managed to graduate at the top of the class. Besides the training program, which took place at the Mission headquarters, I did house to house visitation, street corner preaching, and tract distribution. I worked in the five boroughs of New York, but primarily out of Manhattan, where the Mission headquarters were located.

The Americanization of Eliezer Urbach, together with the new calling, provided exciting, and for the most part, pleasant experiences. There were also humbling and hazardous moments in the acculturation process, but compared to my former life, the "worst" times seemed rather insignificant to me, although consternation was the lot of my trainers.

At a Mission banquet following graduation from the training program, I was delegated to address the audience, many of whom were visitors and strangers. I discovered that my natural ease as a conversationalist hardly translated into a talent for public speaking. My speech was a disaster. A veteran missionary with ABMJ followed me at the podium, and spent his allotted time repairing my embarrassing delivery.

The next morning, my supervisor, Moishe Rosen, called me into his office. Moishe was rather blunt with his suggestion.

"Eliezer, I don't have to tell you there is a problem that must be fixed. You need to be trained in public speaking. The Board recommends that you enroll in a course at the Dale Carnegie Institute immediately."

I began the course in public speaking during a hot, sweltering summer in New York. I drove from Flushing to Manhattan for six weeks, attending four-hour evening classes with a cross-section of other Americans from different ethnic backgrounds, Irish, Italian, German, and one other talkative Jew. We had a grand time together, and in our socializing after class, the American scene unfolded in various arrays—slang and colloquialisms, fast food restaurants and other cuisine foreign to me, particularly Chinese and Italian dishes. The Jewish classmate partook freely of non-kosher seafoods which I had never tasted.

What became an inside joke among the group began with my custom of responding to an introduction with "Praise the Lord!" The first time this happened, someone countered with, "And pass the ammunition!" Never having heard the American war song by that title, I had no idea what the ensuing laughter was all about. My only acquaintances to that date had been believers who expressed themselves frequently with the phrase, "Praise the Lord!" My testimony fell on deaf ears among the Carnegie school friends, but we enjoyed a convivial relationship despite our different orientation toward the world.

One day our instructor told us to bring a newspaper to class for the next meeting. We assumed that we would be reading the paper for practice in English. Not so.

"Roll up the newspapers you have brought this evening," the teacher began the class, "and choose a partner for our lesson on being emphatic."

The newspapers, it turned out, were for whacking the

podium to emphasize a point made in a debating session. After overcoming our conditioned reticence, we thoroughly enjoyed raising dust and debris in learning how to deliver a speech with "emphasis."

Meanwhile, back at the Mission, my teammate, Martin Klayman, was a jolly fellow, full of jokes, and in addition, he was a gallant disciple of the Lord. Martin eventually helped me to overcome much of the fear and trembling with which I approached every Jewish doorstep.

The hazardous part of my training was initiated one morning when Moishe Rosen drove a station wagon into my driveway and made another urgent request.

"Eliezer, a missionary has to know how to drive a car. Here are the keys to the wagon. Go to driving school and learn to operate it."

I had absolutely no experience to draw upon for this assignment. On my first test after attending driving school, I sideswiped a bus. On the second test, I failed to pass in parallel parking. The instructor recruited someone else to accompany me on a third try, a Jewish man who specialized in problem drivers. He was reading the Stock Market reports when I failed to yield the right-of-way and connected fenders with another car. Shortly after a fourth failure to pass the driving test, a new employee of the Mission, Perrin Cook, came to live with us in order to learn about Jewish culture and ways first hand. Perrin courageously volunteered to teach me how to parallel park, etc., and thanks to his patient instruction, I finally obtained a license on the fifth attempt, and became an American driver.

One early negative experience on the missionary front gave me a moment of doubt that I could fulfill this calling. Accompanied by a young trainee from the Mission on her first assignment, we went to visit a Jewish lady who was erroneously reported to be open to the Gospel. Upon arriving at the apartment, we introduced ourselves, and soon began to tell the lady about the Messiah. At the mention of Jesus' name, her face reddened in anger, and she began to shout epithets at us.

"Hitler took away so many of us," she screamed, "and here you are trying to destroy the rest of us!" A flood of obscenities and curses spewed from her mouth.

My young companion and I retreated from the abuse. The lady had devastated the girl and left me badly shaken. We stopped on the stairway leading down to the street, to pray until we recovered from the vicious verbal assault.

"You realize, Susan, that it is the reproach of Jesus' name that has fallen upon us," I consoled my young co-worker. "Jesus warned His disciples that persecution would be their lot, just as it was His. He told us that we would be hated for His name's sake. Now let's pray: O Lord Jesus, please touch that lady's heart so that in time she may come to know you as her Messiah. Grant us strength and confidence to continue in this work, for your name's sake. Amen!"

This was only the first of many similar encounters that I would experience during the ensuing years. Such incidents are common and to be expected, but rejection and abuse are never easy to endure. In October, 1983, I faced a panel of learned rabbis on a local Denver television station, to discuss the beliefs of Messianic Jews. The rabbis took the tactic most painful to any Jewish believer, insisting that since I had accepted Jesus as the Messiah, I could no longer be considered Jewish. To a European Jew whose life was shattered and nearly extinguished during the Holocaust era, this is a very grievous verdict to bear.

In New York, we first lived in an apartment in Queens, then moved into a house owned by the Mission. We stayed in New York for two years doing full-time missionary work. Still possessing an adventuresome spirit, I was sent out to evangelize where no one else wanted to go. After my sojourn in the Brazilian interior, the asphalt jungle did not intimidate me in the least. Civilization and safety seemed to be reasonably permanent here.

Some time after becoming well-established in New York, I

began to have problems with my vocal cords. I had three operations for polyps in one year. I was recuperating from the third operation in Flushing Meadow when a telephone call came from the Mission headquarters. Sara answered the telephone.

"Hello, Sara, could I speak to Eliezer, please?" the voice said.

"You could if he were able to speak," Sara replied. "He can't use his vocal cords yet. Could I take a message?"

"Of course. Would you tell him that we need a missionary in Denver, Colorado. Ask Eliezer if he would like to go there."

Sara relayed the message to me. On a piece of paper, I scribbled, "Where is Denver?"

The geographical location was communicated back through Sara. On my pad, I wrote, "I'll see if I get a leading in that direction."

Sara and I prayed about going to Denver. We asked the Lord for guidance and waited. Soon we were convinced that it was the Lord's will, and accepted the position.

In July, 1970, we arrived in Denver, to serve the Lord in a multi-faceted ministry among both Jews and Gentiles.

⌘

The Holocaust experience forced me and multitudes of other people to wonder about the nature of God. Although I was spared the suffering of many of my people, I was left feeling desolate, nameless, and homeless. Yet it finally dawned upon me that the hand of God was leading me through sorrow and tribulation to a deeper and fuller knowledge of Himself, a spiritual odyssey which eventually revolutionized my life.

I made no special effort to survive. I simply floated with the tide of circumstances, and lived. I came to believe that God allowed me to live because he had a task for me to do, especially among the "lost sheep of the house of Israel." I was a most unlikely prospect for this work. As a youth, nothing in the synagogue seemed to correspond to my lively spirit. My early religious training did leave an indelible mark on my life, but I could not, for many years, either deny or affirm God's existence. As an adult, I looked for peace unsuccessfully in temporal cities.

At last, I made a genuine contact with God. Or was it vice versa? While in Brazil, I saw the love of God in men and women, expressed in their fervent desire that I should know the Lord, too. I was greatly impressed by the born-again Christians in Israel, and the tenacity of their faith in the face of hostility and intolerance. I am grateful to all those who helped me make my own odyssey to faith, before I became a believer and afterward. All along the way, I met people who strengthened me when I was weak, lifted me up when I fell, and comforted me when I was grieving or discouraged. I owe much to many, but most of all, I am grateful to God for providing a happy ending to my story.

Occasionally, someone asks what response my father might have made to my acceptance of the Messiah Jesus. I have a ready answer because I have given the question much thought myself. I think if I had the opportunity to explain to my father what I believe and what I am doing with my life, he would be extremely happy. Why? Because, you see, his blessing has been fulfilled, not as he would have imagined, to be sure, but fulfilled in fact and in truth.

My father, Heiman Urbach, was a deeply religious, loving, and compassionate man. He lived a long life to see, and died by, the forces of evil that constantly keep our world in bloody chaos. On one hand, it could be said that the evils of our time are proportionate to Christendom's failure to live and propagate the faith it professes. On the other hand, that part of the living Church which manifests the spirit of Jesus, restrains rampant barbarism, and the "gates of hell" will not prevail against it. There is a greater need than ever before for an increased recognition of the Messiah, and of all the spiritual values and truths to which He testifies. These are the same values and truths that I learned in my Torah lessons under my father and grandfather's tutelage. In those lessons, I also learned of Israel's

Messianic expectancy. If he could hear my testimony, at least my father would know that the Messiah I choose to follow does not alienate me from my religious heritage, but has, in fact, restored it to me.

My father heard God speaking of old to our fathers in "many and various ways" by the prophets. I have reason to believe that, had he lived long enough, he might have heard God speaking by a Son. As an Orthodox Jew, he recited the daily morning prayer, one of Maimonides' thirteen articles of faith:

> I believe with perfect faith in the coming of the Messiah, and even though he tarries, I shall wait for him every day.

Perhaps with some prompting from his returned prodigal son, I can imagine my father asking the key question of Jesus of Nazareth: "Are you he who is to come, or shall we look for another?"

Heiman Urbach was not a close-minded conformist to tradition, and he had listened many times to the Polish children's nativity play at Christmas time. It makes me smile to myself now when I think that my father made room for the Manger Child in his inn, in a way he never considered possible.

The peace of the Aaronic blessing was sixteen years in coming to me, and it was fulfilled in a way that I could not have anticipated myself. In time, I heard the Messiah of Israel say to me:

> Peace I leave with you; my peace I give to you; not as the world gives do I give to you. Let not your hearts be troubled, neither let them be afraid.   John 14:27.

When I believed God as He spoke through His Son, the peace of God which passes all understanding filled my life at last. It is my great joy to preach the Gospel of salvation in love to both Jew and Gentile, confident that God has set His seal upon me, and given the Spirit as a guarantee in my heart that I am doing God's will.

✌

What can my life story say to people nearly fifty years removed from the anti-human events that rocked the civilized world and defy explanation yet? Those who have become cynical can find within its pages cameo portraits of many people who manifested the resiliency of the human spirit even when they were left seemingly alone to cope with indescribable injustice and human bestiality that staggers the mind. My story, in particular, demonstrates the power of God to heal, strengthen, and restore a battered body and soul, to remove hatred, enable forgiveness of one's enemies, and to establish peace in the heart. Beyond this, amazingly, the Lord can turn a sore and wounded piece of humanity into a joyful ambassador for His kingdom, even though this mission invites more rejection and persecution.

Unless I could conclude with a compelling message of hope, there would have been little incentive to call up so many painful experiences. I tell you now, let us despair of no age and of no generation while the Lord's day of grace shall last. L'Chaim!

Immigrants to Canada

CHAPTER 18

Poland Postscript

My return to Poland forty-one years after departing there under a cloud of grief and despair was, of course, an intensely emotional experience. I visited all the scenes of my childhood and adolescence, and even found my old "musketeer" friend, Franciszek Kubaczka, who led Jozef Pieter and myself out of our home town during the Nazi blitzkrieg of September 1, 1939. Franciszek had been drafted into the German army, as many young men were in that part of Poland, and was sent to fight the Russians. After the war, he returned to Skoczow, married, and has lived there all these years. He knew I had survived through Helena, my old nanny, with whom I kept in contact until she died.

I also met the lady who had cared for Helena until her death, and was given the letters I had written to Helena from Israel so many years ago. The carefully preserved letters witnessed to Helena's incomparable devotion and the dew of her prayers for me.

Out of some 300 Jews who lived in Skoczow before the war, only two remained, and I shared the testimony of my faith with them. We went to the Jewish cemetery in Skoczow, an untended grassy place with perhaps ten or fifteen gravestones all in a heap. Only one gravesite was well-kept, the burial place of a former schoolmate whose older brother is one of the two Jews left in Skoczow. I said kaddish and cried.

I took several pictures of my old birthplace and home without disturbing the family who resides there. The tree I fell out of as a child is still there, the old stone wall covered with wild greenery that was my hiding place, and the garden plot I tended as a boy remain much as these places were 50 years ago. The house is slightly changed in appearance and needs repair. The surrounding countryside is lush and beautiful as it was, and stirred up only fond, pleasant memories. If the war had not come to dislocate me, I would no doubt be living there now, happily operating the inn as my father's heir.

I went to Cieszyn where I attended high school. Being the "county seat," the court building was located here where I could inquire about my father's property. After much searching, the clerk of the real estate register found the record. To my surprise, the property was still registered in my name as heir, along with the name of a long-since-deceased nephew as co-heir. I was shown the entry of debts against the property, and was given to understand that the inheritance might be reclaimed upon payment of the back debts. The clerk made a copy of the land and house register for me. When I presented the documents in the courthouse back in Skoczow, I was informed that some necessary data was still missing. Hoping to delegate power of attorney to someone who could handle the legalities of reclaiming the property, I sought a notary in Bielsko. To my disappointment, I was told that it was impossible to give power of attorney to anyone but a relative or a lawyer. Unable to provide either, the property situation could not be resolved before leaving Poland, but there is still hope that one day it can be settled.

I visited the remains of the Auschwitz camp where my parents were killed by the Nazis. This was an indescribable, still inconceivable, mind-numbing vista of depraved human ingenuity, harnessed to evil power and satanic ideology. God forbid that the world should ever forget what happened there.

I traveled a great deal around the country, visiting as many Jewish people as could be found, most of them old and ailing in one way or another. I met a goodly number of the loving and compassionate Christians who are caring for my Jewish brethren, and was deeply touched by the dedication of these beautiful Christian people who are so genuinely concerned about the surviving Jewish population in Poland. The enthusiasm and warmth of these believers filled me with a whole new store of memories of my native country and the people that dwell therein.

There is a saying that "you can't go home again." I suppose there is some truth in this, but on the other hand, I just did, and it was a good trip. The Lord is still on His throne, and all will be well.

Offering the Good News

EPILOGUE

Especially to My Jewish Brethren

If you have read this far, I hope you will finish these few pages, and let me speak to you from my heart. A little history first, then my own personal experience as a Jewish believer, and how my Jewish identity is affected by my religious convictions.

Yeshua HaMaschiach (Jesus the Messiah) was a native son of Israel. His first followers were Jews, the Messianic movement His coming precipitated was born in the Jewish homeland, and the age-long Messianic hope He fulfilled was a Jewish hope. Yeshua's credentials exactly conform to all the Old Testament prophecies concerning the Messiah's first advent, life, death, and resurrection. We await His coming again in glory, according to Scripture. Yeshua was the truest and greatest Jew who ever lived. Millions upon millions of Gentiles give Him homage.

My own identity as a Jew became important and meaningful when I accepted the Messiah. I am grateful and proud to be a member of the people whom God chose to bring forth the Savior of the world, and to whom He entrusted His oracles and ordinances for the benefit of all mankind. I understand the awesome responsibility this chosenness imposed, and still imposes, upon us. As a Messianic Jew, I believe that the destiny of the world and the destiny of the Jewish people are irrevocably bound together. The people of Israel will yet become the blessing to all nations and peoples that they were called to be when, sometime in the future, Israel blesses the One who will come again in the name of the Lord. Holy Scripture makes it abundantly clear that God will never forsake His special people, and that He will eventually remove the mysterious veil that clouds Israel's understanding of His redeeming love, expressed so beautifully and perfectly in the Person of Yeshua, Jesus of Nazareth.

Meanwhile, individual Messianic Jews like myself, have been freed from the non-Scriptural customs and traditions of men. At the same time, we are free to cherish any or all of our Jewish heritage after the manner of our Lord Jesus. As a follower of Jesus, I feel that I am a true Jew, and an adherent of the whole Jewish faith which God gave in His word, the combined Old Testament and New Testament. In other words, my Jewishness has been freed and bound simultaneously by God's ultimate word in Messiah Jesus.

As to practice, I follow the scriptural guidelines provided by the Jewish apostles of the first century, walking in love as the Spirit enables me. St. Paul said, "All thing are lawful, but not all things are helpful." He counseled all believers to avoid giving offense to Jews or Greeks or to the Church of God, and to take care that our liberty should not become a stumbling-block to others, nor cause a brother to fall.

A loving liberty is also required of Gentile believers. The conference at Jerusalem (Acts 15:1-29), settled the question of how much of the Mosaic law should be imposed upon Gentile followers of the Messiah. Now the question is often reversed: how much gentilization is required of Jewish believers? Actually, this is not the problem it once was, thanks in part to the increased number and work of Messianic Jews. By our presence and witness, we remind Gentile Christians that they revere the Jewish Scriptures, the Old Testament, as the Holy Word of God. In this sacred book, they learn the Jewish concept of the One, true, holy, and living God, as He revealed Himself first to His chosen people. From God's covenants, oracles, and ordinances given to the Hebrew people, Gentile believers accept the fact of human sin, and the need for atonement by blood sacrifice. Through the missionary activities of first century Jewish disciples and apostles, they learned of God's provision for the forgiveness and remission of sin through His own Paschal Lamb, Jesus of Nazareth, a Jew, and hundreds of millions of Gentiles have accepted His salvation.

Therefore, Jewish and Gentile Christians meet in spirit on common ground. Much of the heritage belongs to both Jew and Gentile. Even though worship traditions and customs vary widely, we are all truly united in the Messiah who is our Commonwealth by faith.

The Gospel message of salvation was fully told in the Old Testament. It awaited only the coming into the world of God's Servant Messiah to become flesh and blood fact. God always meant to redeem His beloved fallen creatures, and the plan for our salvation begins to unfold in the first chapter of Genesis. After the call of our father Abraham, God patiently pursued the Children of Israel through centuries of our repeated rebellion, disobedience, apostasy, and idolatrous wanderings away from His revealed will. Although given all the help we could imagine, the Law, the Prophets, and an elaborate sacrificial system, human sin prevailed in our nature and kept us separated from real communion with our holy God. We could not perfectly keep even the first Commandment, much less 613 Mosaic expansions of the Decalogue. Worse than this, our forefathers lost sight of the purpose for which the Jewish people were called into existence—to be a light to the Gentiles and to all the nations of the world. This is Bible history, and as I came to understand it, my own personal history as well.

But God's steadfast love for us would not let us go, nor would He allow His plan to redeem His creation to be thwarted. That plan was a personal rescue, and was accomplished by the historic personage of Jesus of Nazareth, His Anointed One, the Lion of Judah, the root of Jesse, and David's greater Son.

From Genesis to Malachi, hundreds of prophecies and predictions teach that "Messiah will come." These prophecies become more and more specific in detail, until the entire life of God's Messiah is depicted. The first Jewish apostles evangelized with our own Scriptures, the Old Testament, from which they recognized who Yeshua was. Yeshua Himself had given them this method. He said: "These are my words which I spoke to you, while I was still with you, that everything written about me in the law of Moses and the prophets and the Psalms must be fulfilled." (Luke 24:44). These references encompassed the entire Tenach, the Law, the Prophets, and the Writings.

The rejection of Yeshua as the Messiah by the leadership of Israel resulted in the extension of the "unsearchable riches of Christ" to the Gentiles. The full inclusion of the Jewish people will mean "life from the dead," that is, the redemption of the whole world from the destruction wrought by human rebellion against the will of God.

I would ask only that if any of my readers are still in doubt, please search the Scriptures for yourselves, and "may the God of hope fill you with all joy and peace in believing, so that by the power of the Holy Spirit you may abound in hope." (Romans 15:13).

Eliezer and Sara Urbach